Interesting Mysteries
of the
Modern World

I0415390

Volume II

Written By Adam Leon

ISBN 9781091472525

Written By Adam M. Leon

www.ALSET-ORG.com

Table of Contents

Introduction

Over the past few years, I have worked as one of the top writers for one of the most popular conspiracy theory websites on the internet. This has allowed me to spend the majority of my time, every single day, over the past few years, to look into strange occurrences and instances of unexplainable phenomena coming from all around the world. Though I find the work to be, at times, some of the most stressful topics to research and write about, it's a job that I find to be among some of the most meaningful and important discoveries to look into.

Although I have output more than an article a day on this popular conspiracy theory website since my journey as a researcher in the field of the Supernatural, Paranormal and Extraterrestrial began, I find that there is still a mountain more of otherworldly phenomena occurring every single day for me to continue to research and understand. In a sense, I am publishing these volumes of research to help spread information on many of the topics I have already covered while also helping to go back through and refine many of my most popular articles published in the past.

The sections you will read in this book then are only the best of the best that I have prepared for those of whom that wish to better understand the mysterious stories and strange phenomena that plague our world. This also means that, in the near future, more stories will surface and more articles will need to be written that will eventually find themselves published in future editions and volumes.

I hope then that you find this book to be written in the highest quality one could take to share a wide variety of topics of all different kinds that center around the Supernatural, Extraterrestrial and Paranormal.

This book has been broken down into three major categories to help you, the reader, to find the topics of which you find most interesting. Additionally, any one of the articles can be read in any order that you wish. One could spend an entire day jumping around the contents of this book and learning a wide number of many different things of which all find themselves to be articulating many different theories, witness accounts, strange phenomena and ghostly renditions.

In essence, there is no proper way to read this work as there is no proper way to understand the strange nature of the world around us. One must hold an open mind to the articles provided and come to their own conclusions between what they believe is true and what could be the mysterious nature of the universe throwing us for a loop.

I do my best to help clarify terms when necessary, to help provide insight to context when required and to use well-researched and backed information when possible. Unfortunately, this does mean that, given the nature of the articles, there is still a lot left unknown and a truth that you must find for yourself amidst the evidence told here within this book.

There are very specific topics referenced here that would require me to write an entire book about said topic just to comprehend reasonably enough to use in the context of correlating arguments and future references. Of course, I use these specific topics very sparingly and will take the time to slightly elaborate on their correlation to a given topic referenced within this book. If you do find these topics to be increasingly confusing, do not hesitate to contact me so that I may go back through, elaborate on the piece, add additional clarifications and strengthen the article as necessary. I am not an author of some faceless organization. I pride myself in my ability to maintain a constant contact with witnesses and gathered information while also bringing to light these very important topics that no one seems to want to address.

I have also published a wide variety of books surrounding my own personal theories on the nature of the Supernatural, Extraterrestrial and Paranormal that are somewhat mentioned in this book below. If you are interested in learning more about these theories and topics along with purchasing other books published then be sure to go to WWW.ALSET-ORG.COM and pick up a few copies of my past works.

The goal of these written works is to help fund the establishment of the Advanced Logistics Study of Extraterrestrials (A.L.S.E.T.), of which is a private organization, that focuses on the study of Extraterrestrial evidence, behavior, science and technologies. If that is also something that you might be interested in learning more about and helping with, then be sure to visit the site and pick up a few more copies for friends and family.

Thank you for all the support and I hope you enjoy the

written collection of works below! This is currently the second voume of a series of works published in the past so be sure to check out the other published volumes and share the works where you can!

Supernatural

Credible Bigfoot Encounters

For many decades, people from around the world have been fascinated by the numerous sightings of a large ape-like creature that appears to be more man-like than anything. Commonly referred to as bigfoot or sasquatch, this creature is known for its large stature with common sightings reportedly being from around 10 to 15 feet tall.

Though many might not believe that the creature exists, there is overwhelming evidence of its presence in mountains and forests from all around the world. In this section, we will be covering five of the most credible stories that exist and the amazing levels of evidence that entail them.

Number 1: The Marble Mountain Wilderness Video

Noted as being the longest consecutively filmed footage of the bigfoot creature, the Marble Mountain Wilderness video has been the focus of a wide variety of study, recreations and debate regarding the validity of the evidence and the overwhelming answer that it provides. The video is roughly seven minutes in length and provides striking evidence of a humanoid shape atop a nearby mountain ridge that seems to possess elongated forearms, a large build and stands human-like in appearance.

The footage itself is regarded by Bigfoot specialists as a Class A Sighting, which means that the sighting is described as being a clear sighting in circumstances where misinterpretation or misidentification of other animals can easily be ruled out with greater confidence. This means that, without a doubt, the creature scene in the footage is definitely not any animal of any known kind,
of which is a common explanation that skeptics attempt to use to explain away encounters with the Sasquatch as being nothing more than a bear sighting.

An interesting fact to note is that the evidence of this footage was so compelling that the television show "Finding Bigfoot" dedicated an entire episode to the seven minute footage and spent months recreating each shot and measuring out the size and shape of the sighted creature to prove its incredible stature and validity of evidence as authentic Bigfoot footage. They found that the footage was not edited in any way and when the Finding Bigfoot Team recreated the shots, it was uncovered that the creature would have stood at roughly four feet taller than their tallest cameraman, a size of which came out to be a whopping ten feet tall.

Further measurement analyses of the footage also shows that at the still frame of the creature extending its left arm out the entire way, it comes out to roughly 60 percent of its entire body length, six feet long in total. This percentage is similarly seen in apes and monkeys, making its entire arm span 120 percent of its entire body length, much longer than any normal human ratio. It could very well be that the piece is not only overwhelming evidence of the existence of the Bigfoot creature but that it also provides useful measurements and physiological information about the creature for further study by Bigfoot experts.

Number 2: The Independence Day Bigfoot Footage

Though the person who made the film and the location are both unknown, the Independence Day Bigfoot Footage appears to be one of the most compelling pieces of video evidence of the Sasquatch creature to date. FIlmed in an incredible High definition quality, the video shows what appears to be a large bigfoot creature watching the cameraman in a terrified demeanor as the creature attempts to hide from the camera and get away from the person filming. As the person moves in closer in an attempt to get a clearer image and nearly runs up to the creature, a small child-like Bigfoot creature is seen being picked up and carried by the larger Bigfoot creature.

The child turns to face the camera showing that it is a living creature, not that of a prop design or doll, as the larger Bigfoot runs off with lightning speed holding the scared Bigfoot child. Not only is this video evidence of a hidden ecosystem of these Sasquatch creatures living in what can be be accurately described as small tribes, but it also shows eerily human-like qualities of the creature and its worry for the possible Bigfoot cub that it is carrying. Many skeptics claim that the figure seen in the footage is nothing more than a person wearing a gorilla suit, however, the arm length of the creature fits the 120% body ratio seen in other examples of Bigfoot evidence and the picking up of the child proves that if it was a suit, then the person wearing the suit would have to have elongated forearms that would more than surpass the current world record for body-to-arm ratio.

Number 3: Pennsylvania National Forest Trail Cameras

Back in 2007, in order to track any wildlife nearby while on a hunting trip, hunter Rick Jacobs set up several game trail cameras that he mounted to a variety of trees spanning over a large region of the Pennsylvania National Forest, in the hopes of capturing images of nearby wildlife and potential game.

When he came back to review the images the next day, he found that strange pictures of large ape-like creatures were found roaming around the area. These images were in high quality infrared shots taken when the animals passed by that showed the incredible detail down to the hairs of the creatures, appearing to be not only proof of the Sasquatch, but proof of the entire hidden ecosystem of the Sasquatch kind.

Skeptics argued that the creatures were nothing more than images taken of bears standing on hind legs with a very serious and extremely rare case of late stage Mange, however, other images of the hidden game trail camera caught cubs and bears in the region that were perfectly healthy and so the difference is very noticeable between a possible bear sighting and that of the creature seen in the recovered images.

An interesting thing to note is the fact that the creatures spotted, though similar to the Sasquatch in design, appeared to be much smaller in stature, standing at roughly three to four feet tall. It could very well be that the images recovered could be that of a young Sasquatch cub exploring in the night.

Number 4: The Mississippi Highcliff Video

The Mississippi Highcliff Video has been featured on nearly every Bigfoot website, channel, television show and as the staple of the Bigfoot community's prime example of real video evidence. Not only does expert video analysis prove that all of the video is 100 percent genuine, without any edits, cuts or effects, but the video also holds incredible evidence for the validity of the sighting as the events seen are absolutely impossible to hoax with any kind of makeup, prosthetics or gorilla suit. The video was recorded back in 2013 when a Mississippi local, Josh Highcliff, when hunting on his property, noticed a strange figure standing in one of the larger swamps deep in the less traveled parts of the massive property.

He quickly took out his phone and captured footage of the figure with its back turned towards the camera seemingly swimming in the swamp and facing towards a large tree. To those who believe the figure to be nothing more than a man in the suit, the large Sasquatch suddenly begins peeling off massive pieces of the tree with a tremendous amount of an inhuman level of force as it continues playing in the swamps. As Mr. Highcliff films the strange beast, it begins to stand up and appears to nearly double in size, towering over 10 feet tall, before frightening Mr. Highcliff and sending him quickly running off in the direction that he came.

The original video can still be seen on YouTube as the owner of the footage has asked skeptics to explain what he saw and disprove the large beast to help him move past the event and forget about the traumatizing experience. Interestingly enough, the region in which Josh Highcliff spotted the creature has been a hotspot for Bigfoot sightings and has even spawned local myths of a Skunk Ape, a creature with the face of a skunk and the body of a large ape. Could this local myth of the Skunk Ape be further evidence of the existence of the Sasquatch in the region? The footage itself has been solid evidence for the Bigfoot community and only proves that as higher quality cameras become commonplace for people of all ages, the evidence for the Sasquatch will continue to grow.

Number 5: The Dual Sighting of the Provo Canyon Sasquatch

There are many areas stretching across North America that are often referred to as being hotspots for the sightings of the Sasquatch as reported by the Bigfoot community. According to many Bigfoot experts, these concentrated areas get the highest amount of reports of a Sasquatch creature and can span over the course of several years with recurring sightings of the creature. This appears to be the case when analyzing the footage taken on two separate occasions by two separate individuals at the exact same location in the Utah Hills near Provo Canyon.

Back in early 2012, a hiker noticed a large Sasquatch creature sitting on the side of the hill and seemingly playing with a small tree. He quickly turned on his camera and made a noise which caused the Sasquatch to stand up, attempt to hide behind the thin trees and begin throwing rocks at the cameraman. Many Bigfoot experts claim the footage to be genuine given the elongated arms indicating that the creature could not have been a man in a suit due to the fact that it picks up large rocks and throws them a great distance, a behavior reported in many other Bigfoot encounters. Shortly after, the cameraman begins running away in fear of the Bigfoot creature.

Interestingly enough, a few months later in October of 2012, in the exact same spot, a brother and a sister spotted a large furry beast sitting on the side of the hill and took out their cameras to film the creature, believing it to be a large black bear. As they got closer, the creature stood up and began making screeches similar to that of a large gorilla. Though the footage lasts no more than a minute, the quality of the video evidence shows the exact same location as the previous footage and shows the creature standing at a towering 10 feet tall. Not only does this help to prove the authenticity of the previous footage, but proves that the area in and around Provo Canyon appears to be a hotspot location for Bigfoot activity.

Future Space Travel Methods

Given the recent incredible advancements that humankind has made over the past few decades, it appears to be a developing realization that, quite soon, humanity will begin its long and perilous trek into the vast expanse of outer space. Not only is this an inevitable development for the human race, but it seems to be a philosophy that stems more from necessity than luxury. The longer we postpone the developments of deep space colonization, the longer we risk the existence of the human race and potential apocalyptic scenarios.

These developments, however, are only hindered by our methods of transportation. Once space travel is made far more competent and affordable, it won't take much longer before we begin calling the stars our home. In this section, we will be going over the six different ways human beings will likely be able to travel through space in the near future and when we can expect these developments to occur.

Number 1: The Orion Nuclear Space Craft Project

Back during the height of the Cold War and the need for the justification of nuclear testing and nuclear developments, the National Aeronautics and Space Administration (N.A.S.A.) began looking at the amount of energy produced from a nuclear weapon. The administration believed that a nuclear device could be applied to the use of developing spacecraft of which could be capable of traveling large distances in a short amount of time using this exceptional force and energy released by a nuclear explosion in space. Further developments into this study was known as the Orion Project and was at the center of incredible visions of interstellar travel and deep space colonization.

The program was aimed at not only creating spacecraft that could easily be powered by perfectly timed nuclear explosions but also at the effort of sending teams of manned missions to nearby stars and planetary systems at neck-breaking speeds. These speeds would be equivalent to

10 percent the speed of light, ultimately assisting humankind and allowing us to see human colonization of far away planets in as little as one generation. The goal was for the rocket to use basic launching techniques of standard hydrogen-based fuel to break Earth's atmosphere and then for the use of nuclear technologies to be used only in space to prevent the buildup of nuclear fallout on launch pads.

Physics in math and simulations shows that with the efforts used and the designs currently established, a team could make it to the star system Alpha Centauri in a mere 44 years and that missions to nearby planets in the solar system, such as that to Mars, could be accomplished in as little as 30 days with the majority of the time being caused by the warming up and slowing down of the spacecraft. Without taking these factors into consideration, one could theoretically reach Mars in as little as 30 minutes. Unfortunately, all efforts to create the spacecraft were ended shortly after the signing of the Partial Nuclear Test Ban Treaty in 1963.

Number 2: The Light Railway

Elon Musk has challenged modern day corporations and even the National Aeronautics and Space Administration with his revolutionary advancements in the treatment of reusable and affordable spacecraft. Often times, he finds himself arguing that the advancements in spacecraft today will help to shape the industries of the future and the human colonization efforts of neighboring planets. This can only be accomplished, however, if one helps to perfect the transportation methods used via two neighboring planets similar to that of the industrial revolution and the introduction of railroads for shipped cargo, raw materials and transportation.

Interestingly enough, efforts into a new type of space transportation known as a Light Railway could be the way this potential space railroad is achieved in the near future. Research and testing have shown that even when it comes to launching a spacecraft from the surface of the Earth, it is possible to shoot a high powered laser at a simple reflecting device on the craft to generate enough lift and thrust to propel a space craft into the upper atmosphere and far enough into orbit or beyond. Considering the fact that modern day spacecraft uses large solar sails to help propel themselves a great distance using the light emitted from the sun, it is no wonder that this technology appears to be one of the main focuses of private space agencies as well as the National Aeronautics and Space Administration.

In fact, if large lasers are established in space, that harnesses the power of our sun, we can use an immense amount of focused photons to power a strong enough laser to propel spacecraft as far as we see fit. Coupled with a growing velocity that will only compound in the vacuum of space, the energy introduced and used via this Light Railway will be among the most powerful laser technologies ever seen in the history of humanity. Not only is the energy completely renewable but it could also help to prevent the need for the calculation of weight added due to fuel aboard spacecraft and could prove to be a far cheaper and inexpensive method of Light Railway space travel.

Number 3: Photonic Teleportation

Ever since Albert Einstein made his revolutionary scientific discovery relative to the creation of Matter and the fact that Energy is equal to Matter multiplied by the Speed of Light squared, theoretical physicists have come to the realization that all matter in the universe is nothing more than a collection of photons and energy. This means that every building block in your body, every single atom, is nothing more than the grouping of photons that have clumped together. This has led researchers to believe that it is theoretically possible for photonic teleportation to exist in the sense that if a person's body was broken down into nothing but photons, they could be sent at the speed of light to any distance and then reassembled at the other side as if having traveled that distance without any assisted mechanisms of any kind.

This could mean then that the future of space travel could be accomplished by using nothing more than photonic teleportation devices that break down our physical bodies into light, send us across a specified distance at the speed of light and then rebuild us once we arrived at our destination. Not only would this allow us to travel great distances without aging, but we would be able to do so at speeds impossible to attain using any conventional means established.

Number 4: Warp Speed Technologies

Back in 2014, the Laser Interferometer Gravitational Wave Observatory discovered the existence of gravitational waves that naturally occured within our universe. Although gravitational waves were widely disputed by theoretical physicists as being nonexistent and that the sheer idea of such a force violates the fundamental forces of the universe, it appears that previously held notions have been shattered with the LIGO discovery. Not only does this mean that faster-than-light travel is possible, within our universe, but that we have known mechanisms of how to achieve such a feat.

Though the creation of warp technologies would require us to create a binary system of black holes, considering the fact that it is now known to be entirely possible to travel faster than the speed of light within our universe, this revolutionary breakthrough could be the last key we needed to attain the impossible. Efforts to better understand this warp phenomenon have already been well underway and plans to create such Warp-Speed devices seem to be at the forefront of objectives for space agencies of all kind. Very soon, with these recent advancements, we will be able to see the usage of technologies only ever previously written about and entertained in science fiction genres.

Number 5: Instantaneous Transportation

Though evidence of this being able to occur in our universe has yet to be proven, according to the efforts made in understanding gravitational waves and the warping of space and time, Einstein came across a strange revelation when it came to understanding the nature of distance in the universe. It was originally believed, in classical physics, that the shortest possible distance between two points was that of a straight line drawn between both points; however, Einstein challenged this idea by noting that the very fabric of space and time could warp and bend meaning that the shortest distance between two points is rather the two points being directly folded on top of each other.

His analogy was often compared to a worm and an apple. Rather than going around the surface of the apple to get to the other side, the worm could burrow through the apple, creating a hole in the surface and appearing directly on the other side. It is of no surprise then that this theoretical tear through the fabric of space and time is referred to that of a Wormhole. This means that if properly achieved, movement across the universe could be shortened to something known as Instantaneous Transportation. This means that rather than traveling any distance whatsoever, theoretically, one would have to travel no distance at all to seemingly magically appear at their desired location any distance across the universe. Once the mechanisms for how such a movement is achieved, it would be possible that to travel between planets, we would not even have to exit the atmosphere to appear on the other side of the universe.

Number 6: The Usage of Time Travel

After the discovery of gravitational waves made by the L.I.G.O. institute previously covered in the warp speed technologies, there has been a peak revelation when it comes to faster-than-light capabilities and what it means for the future of our species. If it is possible to travel faster than the speed of light, this could mean that the ability to travel through time is also achievable. Time travel could then be used to travel through the 4th dimensional axis of the fabric of space and time to allow us to go to a period in which the universe was much smaller and use that as the plane of movement to move great distances in our time. Meaning that not only would our species be able to experience the incredible insight of time travel, but that it could be the very mechanism necessary to travel all throughout space and time within the blink of an eye.

Monsters Living
In The Mountains

Some of the most unexplored regions in the world are the mountains that can inhabit some of the most populated countries. This is due to the overgrown wildlife, impossible to pass terrain and the overwhelming danger of overcoming one of the biggest obstacles in nature. This has also led many to conclude that there are strange, otherworldly beings that can inhabit these locations, hiding away from civilization and contributing to many of the worlds encounters with unexplainable phenomenon. In this section, we will be going over five different mountain monsters that allegedly roam mountain sides from across the world and what their sightings teach us about the creature.

Number 1: Sasquatch / Yeti

All around the world are strange reports of large ape-like humans that are referred to by locals as Sasquatch, Bigfoot, or the elusive Yeti. At the height of the Yeti craze and the fascination the public had on the strange and elusive creature, the Daily Mail worked to gather their own evidence and make cutting edge reports on finding the creature themselves. After only three years since photographs documenting the existence of the creature were taken by Eric Shipton, a key figure in the search for the Yeti, the Daily Mail sent out an expedition team on the 19th of March in 1954 to journey into the same area the hikers had discovered compelling evidence of the creature and begin their research into uncovering the truth of the creation.

The research team found strange evidence of the native local population having symbolic paintings of the Yeti as well as myths as to what it could be with many of the locals even claiming to have seen the creature on their hikes. When the mountaineering leader, John Angelo Jackson, made the trek up the mountain, he photographed overwhelming evidence of different unidentifiable tracks of flattened footprints from what appeared to be a large biped. These photographs, however, paled in comparison to the evidence the research team would soon uncover in their efforts to prove the existence of the creature.

As they further investigated local myths and legends amongst the population at the base of the mountain, it appeared that as the locals warmed up to the researchers inquiries, they began to reveal to them the evidence they had gathered of the creature on their own.

The researchers were then taken to a Pangboche Monastery in the region and were told by those who lived there that they were in possession of the removed scalp from one of the Yeti creatures. The monastery then allowed the researchers to take the scalp back home for further scientific examinations that were made by Dr. Biswamoy Biswas. The doctor found conclusive evidence that the scalp belonged to no known animal at the time of its finding and that it was not taken from an ape or bear anywhere near the region. Unfortunately, DNA evidence could not be taken from the specimen as an unknown individual had the scalp completely bleached and all the remains of the scalp are a collection of cut up hairs that can only be examined microscopically.

Number 2: The Devil Dog
Of Logan County

Described to share a similar appearance to that of a terrifyingly massive and territorial canine species, the Devil Dog of Logan County has been at the center of a number of strange reports in the area located close to that of the Appalachian Mountains in the United States. Many witnesses in the area claimed to not only have encountered the strange creature when tending to livestock, but that the creature had the supernatural ability of biting into a livestock animal and being able to completely drain the creature of blood similar to that of a vampire. Many have pointed to the strange coincidences this creature has to the Chupacabra, a similar supernatural beast that looks similar to that of a dog and has been known to completely drain the blood out of an animal.

Since the 1930's, witness reports in the region have been consistent with the size and shape of the beast that claim the Devil Dog is somewhere between 3 to 4 feet tall when it is down on all four legs and that it's similar to the weight of a large bear. Evidence has also been found surrounding the Devil Dog of Logan County including massive canine bite marks in trees, recovered drained livestock and witness sightings detailing the beast in detail. Some have even reported that these creatures can hunt and move in packs and have been seen out in the denser regions of the mountains through the brush of trees capable of running at exceptionally high speeds throughout the region. Currently, there has been no reported case of attack from the creature though there are many that go missing all throughout the region every single year. This has led to locals believing that these Devil Dogs are more than responsible for these strange disappearances and the attacks on their livestock.

Number 3: The Snallygaster

Although the creature might seem like a strange amalgamation of many different mythological creatures all put into one, the sightings behind that of the Snallygaster creature have been reported since the first German immigrants landed in the area of Central Maryland back in the 1730's. The first witness accounts of the creature came from these isolated German communities that claimed they were being attacked and stalked by a monster they referred to as the Schneller Geist of which later became Snallygaster to the other immigrants in the region. Witnesses described the monster as having the features of a bird, the features of a siren, and the nightmarish designs of a demon and a ghoul mixed in one.

The creature was detailed as being half-reptile, half-bird, equipped with a metal beak lined with saw-like teeth, the tentacles of an octopus and had the ability to fly down from the sky and pick up and carry off with its victims. Other stories claimed that the monster was capable of attaching its suction cup tentacles to the face of an individual and slowly suck out all of the blood from their body. Reports of the creature seem to end by the end of the 1700's as many of those in the isolated communities claimed to have used stars with seven points on them to ward off the creature away. The complete disappearance of the creature did not prevent stories of the monster from surfacing all throughout the area through rumors and myth. Back in the early 1900's a local news outlet perpetuated a massive hoax report that detailed the monster attacking citizens all over the town of which eventually caused many different citizens to write letters to Theodore Roosevelt to help hunt down and take down the beast. Ever since this event, mention of the creature has faded away and the Snallygaster is only known as an old myth of a monster in the region.

Number 4: The Flatwoods Monster

Recently made popular once again due to the inclusion of the strange creature in a triple A video game title called *Fallout 76*, the Flatwoods Monster is more than just an enemy A.I. in a video game and is actually seen as one of the most terrifying and deadly monsters to exist in the region. Though many consider the creature to most likely be extra-terrestrial in nature, there is no denying its strange other-worldly appearance and almost supernatural abilities. The legend surrounding the creature goes something as follows:

At approximately 7:15 P.M. on the 12th of September back in 1952, three local boys claimed to see a bright object fly overhead and land on a neighboring property. The boys then warned all of the neighbors nearby and were accompanied by a group of people including a nearby National guardsmen and went to investigate the suspected location of the crashed object to piece together what had happened. When the group climbed up the largest hill in the region, they saw in the distance a pulsating red light in the dense mountainside forest only before being attacked by a strange creature that would soon be referred to as the Flatwoods Monster. Witnesses described the Flatwoods Monster as standing at approximately 10 feet tall, with a round blood-red face, a large pointed hood-like head, eye-like shapes that emitted a greenish orange light and a dark black body that hovered above the ground.

According to the witnesses, as well as those in the region of whom reported seeing the creature, the Flatwoods Monster had the strange ability to instill a terrible sickness into anyone that saw it. Reports vary wildly from some reporting that their throat and mouth began to swell up similar to that of an allergic reaction upon breathing in a weird and unexplainable pungent mist surrounding the creature whereas others claim that they began vomiting profusely and becoming disoriented at the sight of the creature alone. Not much more has been uncovered or explained about the creature since these sightings but investigations have still been ongoing since the sighting back in 1952.

Number 5: The Wampus Beast

The Wampus Beast, also known as the Wampus Cat, derives its origins from an old Cherokee folklore that describes the creature as being a large monster similar to that in look and design of that of a monstrous panther. According to the story, an old Cherokee woman was suspicious of her husband and was curious as to where he was going when he claimed he was out hunting. This then led the woman to take the hide of an animal and go out and spy on her husband. It did not take long for the guards of the tribe to find out what the woman was doing and, believing her to be a spy for other tribes in the region, cursed her with spells to be trapped in the animal hide forever. This turned her into the Wampus Beast leaving her cursed in the form of a large panther to forever stalk the region. Rumors today claim that the Wampus Beast lives in the sewers during the day and so carries with it a horrifyingly repulsive stench.

Mysteries Of The Devil's Sea

Although many might be well aware of the Bermuda Triangle and the numerous strange disappearances surrounding the location, many are not yet aware of the Devil's Sea located near Japan and often described as the Pacific Bermuda Triangle. In this section, we will be going over five different mysteries surrounding the Devil's Sea and what they could mean for the region.

Number 1: The Yokohama Danger Zone

Although many claim that the Devil's Sea and its dangers go back centuries, it appears that the majority of the cases have been fairly recent all throughout the area. What many are not aware of is that before the area was popularly given the name the "Devil's Sea", Japanese government officials were already well aware of the strange danger of the location. In fact, the Yokohama Coast Guard of the region outlined the area as a "danger zone" that was to be avoided at all costs though never elaborated as to why the area was given that classification. Several years later, this Danger Zone would end up resting right in the middle of the Devil's Sea Triangle that sees itself at the center of the strange disappearances. Interestingly enough, despite the area having been given the Danger Zone title, the government attempted to deny that the Devil's Sea had ever been a dangerous area after the myths and rumors of the Devil's Sea began causing a strain on the economic shipping conditions and port docking.

Other books written by skeptic authors such as that from Larry Kusche, of whom published the book "The Bermuda Triangle Mystery Solved", appears to be at the center of conspiracies involving the Japanese government making efforts at debunking the Devil's sea Coincidentally, these works and justifications forget to ever mention the nature of the Yokohama Danger Zone and instead try to spin the story of the region in a way that makes it sound that it was never at the center of government danger reports. Despite these books that claim to debunk the danger of the area, overwhelming

evidence shows there is a much higher chance of a ship disappearing or sinking in the Devil's Sea region than anywhere else
in the world, including that of the Bermuda Triangle.

Number 2: The Disappearance Of Nine Ships

The main cause of the legends of the Devil's Sea was
that of the unexplained disappearance of nine different ships.
Between 1950 and 1954, nine modern ships of that era went
missing, in what was described as perfect weather, of which first
sparked the anomalous properties of the Devil's Sea. This caused
Charles Berlitz, an American paranormal writer, to write about
these unexplainable string of disappearances in his book "The
Bermuda Triangle". This eventually led to the name of the region
being dubbed as the "Devil's Sea". In fear of what the damaging
reputation this book could do to the shipping economy of Japan,
Japanese authorities quickly devised a plan as to what could be
done to calm the minds of those fearful of the region.

This led to a wide variety of complete denials from the
Japanese government on the matter, completely rejecting that
the Yokohama Danger Zone ever existed and even giving erroneous reports to the 1975 Author Larry Kusche to help promote
the creation of skeptic writings to refute the works of Charles
Berlitz. Some of these reports included information claiming the
weather was terrible on the night of each ship's disappearance,
that the majority of the ships were equipped with damaged or
inferior radio equipment and that the Yokohama Coast Guard
had never declared any area as a dangerous or unsafe zone anywhere near the region of the Devil's Sea.

Fortunately enough, the evidence was stacked against
the Japanese government of which caused them to rethink this
strategy and attempt new ways to solve the issue of the Devil's
Sea and to cover up any additionally fears of the region. This
ultimately led to the Japanese government's decision to send
research vessels out into the region to attempt to explain the
disappearance of these ships and to help provide a reasonable
explanation that would ultimately see the area deemed as both
safe and passable by ships of all kinds. Despite this move, to this
day, the cause of the majority of the nine ships and their disap-

pearance is still completely unknownand no new evidence from 1975 has ever helped to explain where the ships could be and what happened to them.

Number 3: The Sinking Of The Kaiyo Maru No 5

In an effort made by the Japanese government to dispel the myths of the region that, at this point in time, was more than affecting the economy of the nearby ports and harbors, a research vessel by the name of the Kaiyo Maru Number 5 was sent out to understand the underlying cause of the disappearance of the many different ships that had ventured in the area. The Japanese government was more than confident that the ship would return with the discovery of the sunken ships in the region or new insight as to what could potentially be causing the sinking of the ships. Additionally, by sending out a state-of-the-art research vessel in the region without worrying about the supposed dangers of the Devil's Sea, the Japanese government believed this would more than overwhelmingly convince ships that the area was safe and capable of being used for passage and ease of imports.

Unfortunately, however, it appears that the sending of the research vessel, the Kaiyo Maru Number 5, had quite the opposite effect of what was expected by the government. It appeared rather quickly that the ship had been been destroyed and/or lost in the region of the Devil's Sea almost immediately upon beginning its journey in the region and studying the strange phenomenon of the location. This only led to the solidification of the fears that surrounded the nearly supernatural dangers of the Devil's Sea and what it could mean for any vessel that passed through the region. It would not be for another few decades before the cause of the disappearance of the scientific research vessel known as the Kaiyo Maru Number 5 and its crew of 100 personnel would be uncovered.

Number 4: Recent Discovery Of Methane Concentrates

Despite skeptics and their constant arguments that the area was not at the center of any irrational dangers, researchers would later uncover the truth as to the nature of the area and its nearly impossible to believe natural phenomenon that could sink ships without a second's thought. It appears that, for some unknown reason, the area seems to hold a large amount of pressure of methane gases that become cencrated in a region and act similar to that of timed explosions.

There appears to be a large number of fields all across the Devil's Sea of Methane Hydrates that seem to form for some unexplained reason. These Methane Hydrate gases can spontaneously explode if the temperature surrounding the area slightly rises to 18 degrees celsius. It has been theorized that there seems to be a potential for these explosions to cause an interruption in buoyancy in the surrounding areas that could very easily sink a ship overhead, leaving behind no trace of the debris.

In this sense, the area seems to act like a naturally forming minefield that seems to replenish itself every now and again after a large amount of eruptions form. This strange and unexplained natural phenomenon then led to the sinking of any vessels caught in the region at the moment of this event. It appears overwhelmingly that despite what the skeptics claimed and the governments had denied in the past, there is obvious reason to believe that the region is far more than dangerous given these naturally forming minefields of Methane Hydrate gases.

Number 5: Strange Underwater Volcanic Pressure

Alongside the evidence of the methane concentrates and underwater pressure, researchers also uncovered additional evidence of a super massive underwater volcano in the area of the Devil's Sea. These large volcanoes have been discovered in the past to be able to erupt at sporadic times and even cause instances of seismic activity in the oceans nearby that of Japan that could create miniature tsunamis and large waves throughout the region even during a seemingly perfectly weathered day. This has led researchers to believe that the underwater supermassive volcano could also be at the center of the formation of these Methane Hydrate gases all throughout the region and other strange anomalies reported throughout the Devil's Sea, such as that of glowing light underwater, sudden waves and boiling spots.

Oddly enough, this underwater volcano and sudden seismic activity has even led to the appearance of new islands in the region along with the disappearance of old islands in the area that sees the Devil's Sea at the center of a rapid creation and destruction of islands all throughout its location. In fact, the formation and destruction of the islands appears to be so rapid that many of these islands will never be seen in satellite imaging and will never have been known to exist in the first place before being wiped away from existence.

Additionally, evidence of the sinking of the Kaiyo Maru No 5 was tied to that of an underwater volcanic eruption in the region of the Devil's Sea that it was supposedly focused on researching under orders of the Japanese Government. Although no exact information could be gathered as to how it was sunken or destroyed, many still feel confident that the volcanic eruptions in the region are more than enough to capsize such a vessel. Ultimately proving that the area of the Devil's Sea is a strange and anomalous region that appears to be both incredibly dangerous and nearly impossible to understand.

Radio Signals From Space

The vastness of space has left it to be one of the last unexplainable frontiers of the human race. With it has also come a wide number of strange and anomalous properties that, even the most well-versed experts on the matter, can't explain. Such phenomenons include strange signals, unexplainable behavior of stars and that of impossible-to-detect radiation far out of the reach of humanity. In this section, we will be going over five different mysterious and unexplainable radio signals that scientists have received from deep space and what it could mean for the future of humanity.

Number 1: The Music Of Saturn

As the Cassini Mission saw its final orbits around the gas giant, Saturn, it began using its state-of-the-art equipment to gather as much data of the planet as it could before leaving it behind, forever. This gathering of information included the electromagnetic wave data acquired from the waves of plasma moving from Saturn to its moon, the Enceladus. This plasma wave seemed to be similar in nature to that of a radio signal translated from electromagnetic information in music and so when researchers decided to translate the information into that of a radio signal, they came upon a strange discovery.

The signal seemed to sound eerily familiar to that of long dragged-out chords of music. The recording of this strange phenomenon was first made on the 2nd of September, back in 2017, by an instrument known as the Radio Plasma Wave Science Instrument. Experts hope that this gathering of information will help to shed light on the appearance of these plasma waves and their movement that seems to be caused by a variety of unknown factors.

Today, you can still hear these Cassini recordings that many describe as both a creepy and unsettling noise. Given the fact that the cause of these naturally forming plasma waves are entirely unknown, it appears that scientists are still struggling to come up with answers for this weird occurrence for Saturn and its moon, the Enceladus, and will soon be attempting to gather future information in other space missions as to the nature of the gas giant and its surrounding celestial bodies.

Number 2: Radio Bursts 3 Billion Light Years Away

Something, somewhere, out deep in the vastness of space is some strange anomalous mystery object that continues to throw extremely large blasts of radio waves out from around it in all directions, travelling at the speed of light. Fast Radio Bursts (FRBs) have always been a mystery for astronomers and scientists in the field trying to understand the strange nature of the cosmos, but this new finding might help to shed light onto what might be causing these strange signals. When astronomers turned their attention to the possible source of these FRBs, they discovered an area with an extremely strong magnetic field; ultimately suggesting that these FRBs come from an unexplainable object that exists in a very intense galactic environment containing an extremely strong magnetic source. Scientists are still trying to understand what could be causing this extreme magnetic source and not many theories have arisen since its discovery back in January of 2018.

The lead researcher on the matter, Emily Petroff, working out of the Netherlands Institute for Radio Astronomy claimed that researchers are directly probing the local environment of a source in a distant galaxy said to be responsible for this matter more than 3.8 billion light years away. The current theory of the cause is said to be that of a supermassive black hole that might be affecting a nearby entity causing the source of the magnetism, though any additional information is completely unclear on the matter.

Still, it appears that the team is hard at work attempting to gather as much information as they can that has led them to the theory of a possible supermassive black hole, a nearby neutron star and possible gas tendrils from the area. The research group is confident that in a few years, more creative theories will emerge to help explain this strange radio anomaly coming from deep space and what it could mean for the extreme local galactic environment.

Number 3: The Wow Signal

Before the establishment of the SETI project in 1973, the only radio telescope working to uncover the mystery of extraterrestrial life was that of Ohio State University's Big Ear Radio Observatory that was turned on back in 1963 and had the sole purpose of listening out in the cosmos for extraterrestrial signals.

The strange thing was that 14 years after it was first turned on, it received a signal that most members of the alien community deem the most substantial piece of evidence for extraterrestrial life regarding the S.E.T.I. project involving radio telescopes. On the 15th of August in 1977, a 72 second long transmission was captured while the Big Ear telescope was pointed towards the constellation Sagittarius that bore the expected hallmarks of extraterrestrial origin.

In fact, prior to this event, back in 1959, researchers posited forth the theory that if extraterrestrial contact was ever made, it would most likely be of that in the radio wave frequency of 1420 megahertz, of which is the specific frequency naturally emitted by hydrogen, the most common element in the universe and therefore likely familiar to all technologically advanced civilizations.

Oddly enough, the 72 second long transmission was exactly within the 1420 megahertz frequency with peaks and lows exactly equal to each other in variation marking that not only was this a mathematically symmetrical frequency, but that there was no possible way that this frequency could have a non-artificial origin.

This 72 second transmission was then given the title of the WOW Signal, of which was named after the lead researcher of whom discovered the signal in the data and wrote the small side note of "Wow!" to indicate the unbelievable nature of the data. Skeptics and researchers to this day have had massive difficulty trying to explain away what this signal could have originated from and so it could very well be that on a lonely planet out in the Sagittarius constellation, we heard the radio signal of a greeting more than 25,000 light years away.

Number 4: The Space Roar

Back in 2009, top researchers at the Goddard Space Flight Center sent a device up into space via a giant balloon known as ARCADE. ARCADE was an acronym that stood for Absolute Radiometer for Cosmology, Astrophysics and Diffuse Emissions, of which details its mission as being that of a searching device capable of picking up diffuse radiation caused by the universe's earliest stars. It was a huge surprise then that instead of picking up these weak signals, the ARCADE device captured data that scientists have described as a space roar. Although a large amount of radio waves caused via synchrotron radiation was expected by researchers at the Goddard Space Flight Center, what was recovered and analyzed turned out to be radio waves six times the normal amount expected to be heard as well as their origin points being from that of galaxies 2.5 million light years away.

This had led many to speculate the possibility that perhaps this enormous amount of background radio waves found in our universe could be that of extraterrestrial civilizations and their frequencies sent out into the vacuum of space. This could very well be the case considering our radio wave frequencies have been spreading out like a bubble from earth since the first transmissions were sent a little over 100 years ago and, given the fact that these extraterrestrial civilizations could predate us by millions of years, we could be picking up the faintest signals that have reached us over a vast distance of both space and time. Scientists struggle to find any other cause for this mystery and have left many wondering if whether or not we are truly alone in the universe or we are merely the latest species to tune in to an age-old galactic conversation.

Number 5: The First Radio Broadcast

Though its influence in history has been astounding, the small broadcasting device we know as the radio has not been around for very long. In fact, its inventor, Nikola Tesla, did not first conceive of the device until 1885. Despite the young age of the device, it was made apparent that Mr. Tesla was far ahead of his own time when first coming up with its invention, being the only inventor of his time to be made aware of the electromagnetic spectrum and the ability to tap into its powers and uses. Oddly enough, Tesla wrote extensively in his notes that when he made the first radio capable of receiving and broadcasting his signal, as soon as he turned on the device, he could already hear another person's voice on the other side. He would later go on to claim that the people transmitting him a signal were those of beings living on the surface of Mars and that they were attempting to make first contact with him.

This was only made more eerie as Nikola Tesla wrote that this voice was that of a man calling out his name, saying "Tesla. 1. 2. 3." over and over again before the signal cut out entirely. Many researchers speculate that this signal could have been nothing more than background radiation misinterpreted by the inventor that was caused by a solar wind of the sun; however, many believe that perhaps something far more creepy could have been going on in the background. No explanation for this strange occurrence has been provided and still many more speculate that perhaps Nikola Tesla made contact with something not quite human. Ranging from extraterrestrials to time travelers, the conspiracy theory community seems hellbent on trying to discover the root cause of Nikola Tesla's first received broadcasts.

Secret Military Bases

The world is clouded with secret agendas and government conspiracies. It is not a wonder then that there are secret and hidden military bases with clearances so top secret that even getting close to the general area of the base could lead to government action and military arrests. In this section, we are going to cover five mysterious military bases that no one is allowed to visit and why that may be.

Number 1: Area 51

Often detailed in pop culture references as a testing grounds for alien technologies, the United States military base located in Lincoln County, Nevada, is an especially mysterious air force base. Not only are the majority of projects held at this military base regarded as black budget projects, but clearance just to get near the military base is an impossible task that even the most influential reporters have issues overcoming.

Satellite imaging of the base itself is believed to be edited and tampered with and, considering it is quite nearly impossible to get reliable footage of areas even surrounding the military base, the contents inside its safely protected border are still a mystery to the general public.

During the 1950's, the Roswell incident caused a massive information leak from the military base of which made claims of a crashed unidentified flying object being taken to Area 51 to be studied and reverse engineered. Interestingly enough, even then United States President, Eisenhower, found it incredibly difficult to gain clearance to enter the military base. Records of letters of worry and requests for information written by the president were completely ignored by the air force base and the research scientists stationed there.

Number 2: Royal Air Force Rudlow Manor

Found to be at the center of many different alien conspiracies and mysterious leaked information, the Royal Air Force Base at Rudlow Manor was officially described and used as an operations and intelligence military base during its earliest conception. This plan soon changed as new developments across the manor took place.

After the creation of vast complex tunnels and private contracts for developments in the fields of unidentified flying objects, the military base began becoming synonymous with secrecy and clandestine operations. These claims only further metastasized when declassified documents released at the National Archives outlined and indicated that the site was a center for Unidentified Flying Object testing and alien investigations throughout the 1950's.

This secrecy even extended above the clearance of most British politicians and found that the information contained within the base to be at the highest clearance level imaginable, even found to be above most clearances for agents within secret intelligence services and high positions among the British military.

Current information on the accurate descriptions of on-going projects at the military base are wrapped in further secrecy as most declassified files regarding the location are over six decades old. Providing no further insight into current investigations and military projects at the Manor.

Number 3: Diego Garcia

Diego Garcia is a military base so secretive that information regarding the location is merely seen as rumor and has proven to be hardly reliable. The United States Military facility is located in the Indian Ocean on the island of Diego Garcia and in most leaked documents, is described as an example of the dangers of secrecy.

Known for removing indigenous populations to breaking rules outlined in the United Nations Charter, this military base is more than just a secret, it's a cover up. Many contract workers that worked for private companies on the island to help build and develop the military base have provided witness statements and proof of activity on the island that seems both mysterious and strange in nature. In fact, many of these actions caused scrutiny from international efforts after examining reports of workers from private contract firms not being paid or being given a month's salary of six U.S. Dollars.

This has led to the military base becoming a multi-billion dollar development and the reason for its existence and further developments clouded in mystery. Given its scrutiny and international media attention, information regarding the military base has proven to be completely unreliable as false reports were created and leaked to work to cover up the truth of its future developments.

Number 4: Project Iceworm

Project Iceworm was an attempt by the United States government to develop secret nuclear launch sites in remote locations in the iciest places of Greenland. The idea was to place secret networked launch sites under the ice that would be unable to be spotted by counter-surveillance technologies due to consistently terrible weather conditions and remote geographical features. The code name was a top secret reference hidden under the highest levels of clearance and declassified in only recent years. To cover up the creation of these potential nuclear launch sites, the United States Army created a highly publicized project called Camp Century, whose goal was to merely study ice, different forms of ice and the structural stability of glaciers.

Interestingly enough, this obviously terrible lie worked for the governments of that region and its true purposes in the project was known only by high military officials working under top secret clearances. Designs for the secret networked military base outline incredible levels of detail when it came to the study and formation of a military base under the ice but deemed the project to be too unsafe due to structural failings of glacial ice.

This lead to Project Iceworm becoming supposedly cancelled in 1966 and the idea of a nuclear launch site being formed under the ice completely abandoned by the U.S. Military. However, new leaked documents outline a possible cover up of this finding. Diagrams and detailed blueprints give credence to the theory that the United States Military and Top Secret officials built complex mobile nuclear power plants, mobile bases and mobile launch sites that held the capability of moving with the rotating glaciers and could possibly exist in undisclosed locations in Greenland.

Continuing down into the complex information released in these leaked documents, it was detailed that a secret mobile United States military base had already been constructed. The outlined information claimed that the launch complex floors would be 28 feet below that of the surface of the ice and that the entire surface area of the secret military base exceeded 52,000 square miles in deep tunnels and underground facilities. This size being roughly three times the size of Denmark.

Current information on the matter has been silenced and future leaked documents have yet to arise. There is no information outside of this development and the existence of such a base is still highly questioned.

Number 5: Unknown Russian Military Base

On January 15th, 1965, the Russian government created Lake Chagan by using a nuclear device to create a wide enough crater to hold water distributed by the nearby river known by the locals as the Chagan River. The official disclosure regarding the creation of the lake by the Russian government was to create a reservoir of water that could be delivered to nearby towns and promote peaceful nuclear developments.

The Project was titled "N.E.N.E." for the belief of nuclear developments that could benefit the Russian National Economy and prove as effective propaganda that nuclear devices can be used for positive means and not just as instruments of war.

Oddly enough, the project's justification and continued means seemed questionable, but none more so questionable than the events surrounding the developments of Chagan Lake. The justification of the lake being created for the sole purpose of storing water to be used by nearby populations did not seem to hold merit as the lake was quickly deemed unsafe and uninhabitable. The potential for it to be used as drinking water was quickly dismissed and the developments for creating a channel or method of delivery for the water in the reservoir was completely nonexistent. Not only this, but there were no nearby populations to benefit from a sudden creation of a drinking water system as the creation of Chagan Lake found it to be roughly in the middle of nowhere and completely out of distance of nearby populations at the time.

Even more surprising is the lack of overall consistency in information regarding reports of the logic of its creation which has begged further questioning and investigations from conspiracy theorists that wish to uncover the truth.

Made in a recent discovery of archived russian footage surrounding the creation of Chagan Lake shows split second images of a secret Russian military base or research outpost in the area at the time of the lakes development. This has led investigators to believe that there was a tremendous cover up that took place with the creation of Chagan Lake and that a potential secret military base could have been the original reason for the need of this cover up. In fact, there are no Russian documents, references or further information surrounding this supposed military base at its location and is believed to be so incredibly top secret that it may have housed beings that were supernatural, paranormal or extraterrestrial in nature.

Given that the only proof and evidence of the existence of the Russian base is 3 frames of images from an old faded archived footage of the creation of the lake, it is impossible to say if this secret base truly exists. If it does, however, it would be one of the greatest cover ups and top secret military bases the world has ever known of.

Strange Anomalies
In The Ocean

It is true that we know more about what is going on, on the surface of the moon than what is happening within our very own oceans on planet Earth. Seen as one of the most unexplored areas of the planet, our oceans are teeming with incredible mysteries and strange occurrences that have left experts all around the world baffled and amazed since their discoveries. In this section, we will be discussing these strange mysterious in detail as we uncover five different instances of mysterious anomalies discovered in the ocean's of our world.

Number 1: An 8.5 Mile Pyramid Discovered Underwater

Back in 2016, a strange and unexplainable deep sea anomaly was discovered. Spotted using state-of-the-art satellite information, there appears to be a massive pyramid construction underwater that completely dwarfs the size of the Pyramids seen at Giza. It appears that the structure seems to be somewhere around 3.5 to 11 miles across and looks to be resting in a large area of underwater terrain in the Pacific Ocean, a little west of Mexico. Many can even view the massive structure using Google Earth satellite images when looking up the coordinates at 12 Degrees North at 119 Degrees West.

The discovery of the object was made by a researcher located out in Argentina, by the name of Marcelo Igazusta. He claims that the structure could be evidence of the formation of an ancient civilization long before man was supposedly capable of roaming the planet and that, at a different time in Earth's history, could have experienced a change in tide that would allow the construction of the monstrosity. His theories, however, have not prevented a wide range of conspiracy theories from forming in the community.

Many believe that it could very well be a possibility that the structure isn't that of a large underwater pyramid, but that of a secret alien base inhabiting the ocean floor. Many have often referenced the existence of strange sightings of Unidentified

Submerged Objects or that of UFO's exiting from under the ocean and shooting off into the sky in different maritime accounts. Given the structures massive size, sudden appearance and strange artificial shape, this has led many to undoubtedly believe that it appears to be of extraterrestrial origin.

Interestingly enough, other researchers have picked up on the discovery and well-known alien hunter, Scott C. Waring, has already posted in his blog, "UFO Sightings Daily" that an 8.5 mile estimate is only a conservative estimate and that the true size of the discovery could be somewhere north of 11 miles across and possibly grouped up with other impossible to see structures in the region.

Number 2: Grid Anomaly Found On Ocean Floor

Back in 2011, an elaborate post was written by a user that noticed strange and unusual ocean floor grid patterns that seemed to be artificial in nature. This grid pattern seemed to span 60 miles in width and 65 miles in length and had numerous different right angles all across its formation. The post then goes on for several more paragraphs talking about how the carving all throughout the area appears to be artificially created with what is described as being similar to that of paved streets, walkways and a number of smaller squares all throughout the region that also seem to have 90 degree angle turns and share a look that is similar to modern day property lots.

At first many rejected the discovery and believed that the entire finding was nothing more than conflicting terrain maps compiled together by satellite data; however, the information surrounding the heights and depths of the terrain was not of that of overlapping or erroneous bugs in the satellite information. Additionally, in the comments following the thread, many others began pointing out similar discoveries of these strange grid like patterns found in many different parts of the ocean as well and what it could potentially mean for the history of humanity or the formation of underwater structures.

To this day, there still appears to be no explanation on

the matter and not a single researcher will comment on the discovery for reasons that are not completely understood. This could very well mean that information surrounding these strange grid-like anomalies could be actively suppressed by governments from around the world or that they could be at the center of top secret missions involving military involvement or extraterrestrial cover up. Unfortunately, we won't be getting any answers for this strange discovery any time soon.

Number 3: Underwater Lake Discovered Under The Ocean

Comedically dubbed with the moniker of the "Hot Tub of Despair", it appears that research scientists have discovered a strange underwater anomaly that can only be described as an underwater lake so toxic that it is viewed as a large biohazard to life throughout the region. The underwater lake rests 3,300 feet below sea level in the Gulf of Mexico and seems to be at the center of a vast desert-like region of the ocean uninhabited by life. The lake appears to be a pit of water that is visibly heavier and more condensed than the surrounding water, giving it the appearance of a naturally forming lake underneath the ocean.

Research scientists have discovered that this lake is filled with extremely salty forms of water, much saltier than the water surrounding it, while being mixed with a rare form of dissolved methane that will instantly kill any sea creature that falls inside. This discovery was made by a research team from San Pedro that used underwater research vessels to help assist with the gathering of information surrounding underwater biology and geology.

Although they were more than surprised by the appearance of the underwater lake and its toxicity, they were well aware of similar phenomenon found all across the world described as brine pools. The discovery of this unique brine pool has helped shed light into the formation of such a phenomenon and the effect it has on surrounding marine biology and their habitat. It appears that an artificial wall of mussels living on the edge of the forming waters helped to keep the underwater lake intact and capable of maintaining its form in the ocean, a behavior never before seen in the region.

Interesting enough, despite this information gathered, it appears that researchers are still studying these occurrences as they find them to be very strange underwater anomalies and rare in nature. If more of these crater-like structures can be discovered in the near future, it might help to shed more light into the unexplainable nature of these underwater lakes and their effect on marine biology.

Number 4: The Bloop And The Julia Sound

Back in 1997, a sound was recorded emanating from deep within the ocean in vast unexplored regions that was so loud that it was actually considered to be one of the loudest sounds on Earth ever recorded. At the time, it was given the nickname the Bloop as the recorded noise mimicked a lot of the sound patterns of marine animals in some ways. The strange thing about this noise was that the sound was so loud, for it to have been a sea creature, it would have to emanate from a marine animal larger than the size of most naturally formed islands.

Because of this impossible size, the national oceanic and atmospheric administration considers the noise to have been caused by a possible icequake, a large shattering sound caused when massive pieces of underwater ice begin cracking; however, many experts reject this explanation as the noise is too loud for standard icequake recordings and so has been seen as a mystery requiring more evidence for explanation.

Oddly enough, the noise would once again resurface years later in 1999. Nicknamed the Julia sound, the recording mimicked the original behaviors of the Bloop recording and was recorded by a number of different devices that helped to analyze the recording in much greater detail, which helped the audio to be determined closer to a cooing sound or a continuous whining noise. This might be definite proof that perhaps rather than icequakes, there appears to be a massive underwater creature deep beneath the ocean's surface.

Interestingly enough, it also appears that new information regarding the matter has recently surfaced due to H.P.

Lovecraft enthusiasts and a collection of conspiracy theory writings. According to the Lovecraftian novels, a large ancient Elder God, known as C'thulhu, rests at the bottom of the ocean awakening to rise one day and bring on the end of humanity. In the book, Lovecraft elaborates and provides a location to the monster as residing somewhere around a Latitude of 50 Degrees South and a longitude of 100 Degrees West. Oddly enough, the source of the Bloop sound had been traced to be at a 50 Degrees South Latitude and a 100 Degree West Longitude, directly matching this Lovecraftian tale.

Number 5: The Baltic Sea Anomaly

During the Summer of 2011, an independent swedish-based organization known as the Ocean X Team began its search for sunken treasures and historical artifacts that could be recovered from old rumored shipwrecks in the region of the Baltic Sea. Interestingly enough, as they continued in their investigation using high end sonar imagery equipment, they soon discovered a strange image taken that appeared to look strikingly similar to a sunken unidentified flying object.

Referred to as the Baltic Sea Anomaly, below the waters appears to be a strange formation that contains sharp edges, a large overall body and an interesting shape that looks similar to that of a large completely circular flying saucer. Unfortunately, no efforts could be made to go deeper into the water and uncover the true nature of the object as the structure appears to be located too deep for an independent research team to explore. Because of this, no new information regarding the structure can be uncovered and the strange Baltic Sea Anomaly is still hidden deep beneath the waters.

Strange Substances Discovered

All around the world, research corporations and major industry developers work around the clock to better understand and uncover materials that could be used to change the nature of our reality and help to improve the industrial market for a better and brighter future. Every now and then, these research efforts tap into a plethora of strange chemical compounds of metallic alloys that demonstrate properties that were never before theorized. In this section, we will be going over these strange and mysterious substances that research scientists have discovered, what they can do and why they are being used in the industry today.

Number 1: Nitrogen Triiodide

Unless you are one of the experts that helped to produce it in the industry, not many can guess what this strange material does when just hearing the name alone. While the word triiodide is often used to refer to a variety of chemicals of which have the ability to be mixed with other chemicals to create different compounds, Nitrogen Triiodide holds a special place for being a strange substance that had surprised the researchers of whom first created it. Nitrogen Triiodide is unbelievably explosive. While most explosives will use chemical processes that rely on either heat or combustion, Nitrogen Triiodide is different in that it is explosive on contact. If the chemical compound touches next to anything, even placing it on a table, it will ignite the compound in a fiery blaze that makes it one of the most incredibly volatile substances in the world. This is caused due to the fact that any amount of friction will set off the volatility of the compound and see it set ablaze.

Number 2: Vantablack

After going viral many years ago when the internet was surprised to see a strange material that was so black that it seemed to be impossible to even look at with the naked eye, many were wondering what material could have been responsible for such a strange phenomenon that led people to even believe photo manipulation was at the center of the effect. This strange material responsible is known as Vantablack and it currently holds the word record for the darkest material on the Earth. Vantablack was originally discovered and manufactured by the Surrey NanoSystems company of whom normally create and work on nanotubing.

Interestingly enough, the properties of Vantablack make it an incredible conductor of heat from photons and can even catch a material on fire if sprayed with the paint version of the material on any object. This is due to the fact that the material allows the retention of 99 percent of all light that hits it. Recently, a building in South Korea was coated in the material to create the darkest place on Earth that can be visited by tourists of whom wish to see the incredible qualities of the material.

Number 3: Ultra Hydrophobic Material

Of course, many people have seen the strange effects of hydrophobic material and how, when it is sprayed or layered across a fabric, it can completely bounce water away from the material without it sinking in at all. This has led to incredible inventions such as hydrophobic coating to protect against water damage, socks that can walk through a lake and not get wet and even metallic parts that seem almost immune to many different forms of rusting.

This is; however, only the tip of the iceberg and, though hydrophobic material might also appear like a strange and otherworldly material, Ultra hydrophobic material is even more than just an unusual material. Ultra Hydrophobic material can turn water into marbles. If you spray any fabric or material with the Ultra Hydrophobic material, you will find that it repels water so well that it will actually encase any amount of water in on itself, causing it to take the form of a marble that will be able to be rolled around in the palm of your hand. The applications for industry are near limitless and, very soon, we might be seeing them applied onto car windshields to prevent the need of buying new windshield wipers every single year.

Number 4: Supercritical Fluid

Under very specific standards of both pressure and temperature, a material could enter what is described as Supercritical Fluid. Supercritical Fluid is caused when a fluid becomes superheated to the point that it is above its critical temperature and pressure. Critical temperature refers to when an object is heated to the point that it cannot liquify and either maintains a solid form or a gaseous form. Because of this change in heat and pressure, the material will rest at a point that is indistinguishable from that of a gas, a liquid or a combination of both. This means that though the state might be in a form similar to that of a gas, it will act and behave similar to that of a liquid as well and seem to possess properties completely impossible to predict.

Number 5: Industry Nickel Titanium

The Nickel Titanium alloy is referred to in the industry by the name of Nitinol. Although most metallic alloys are used in different industries such as that of construction, vehicle design or even in electronic components, Nitinol is different in that it holds a special property making it incredibly useful for that of the medical industry. It appears that, in the way that the alloy itself forms its atomic bonds, it can be built to remember a very specific shape in which it was designed and that, when the alloy is twisted or distorted into a new shape under stress or compression, it can very easily twist itself back into its neutral shape with ease. This allows the material to be used in stents or other practical medical needs as well as industry materials that allow the alloy to twist and contort and them always resume back to its normal shape.

Number 6: Gallium

Similar in property to that of the liquid metal robot seen in the popular science fiction movie Terminator 2: Judgement Day, Gallium appears to be one of the softest metals in the world and has a melting point that allows it to melt just from the heat of your hand. The element itself is bright, shiny and silvery-white in color, making it look very similar to that of Liquid Mercury but does not hold any of the dangerous side effects. In fact, there are many videos showcasing this metal's strange property as people hold the soft metallic piece in their hands and watch it slowly melt like that of a chocolate bar. Even when the material is in its solid form, it is so soft that you could cut it with a butter knife as it holds the consistency of a block of peanut butter.

Number 7: Graphene Aerogel

One of the strangest materials on this planet that almost seems to defy belief is that of the creation of solid objects that are made out of 99.98 percent of air by volume. Graphene aerogel is one of the lightest materials ever created, even holding a density that is lower than that of Helium gas and only slightly higher than Hydrogen. The material was created when researchers took Hydrogel, a consistency similar to that of jelly and replaced all of its liquid counterparts with air. Outside of creating the least dense of all known solid materials, Graphene Aerogel finds its uses in that of fillers, coatings, adhesives and is even being used to develop lightweight 3D printing that can produce incredibly precise leves of results.

Number 8: Starlite Material

Back in the 1970's, appearing on a popular television show known as Tomorrow's World, that showcased incredible inventions and scientific discoveries that would lay the foundation for a better and brighter future, was a revolutionary new discovery known as Starlite. Starlite was an intriguing new chemical compound that demonstrated an incredible ability of heat resistance of all kinds when undergoing testing on the television show. According to many different sources including the NASA spokesman Rudi Narangor, Starlite was capable of defending a material from heats that exceeded 10,000 degrees Fahrenheit.

This was tested using state-of-the-art lasers with an intense and focused beam capable of generating the heat equivalent of the surface of the Sun. Despite this heat being directed at

Starlite for a prolonged period of time against the material, it never penetrated the material and was completely unabsorbed, leaving Starlite cold to the touch immediately upon ceasing the application of heat. The material also proved to be incredibly efficient at dispersing energy and heat commonly seen in nuclear blasts, being more than capable of withstanding the blasting force and the heat generated by such a weapon.

Number 9: Dark Matter

Out of all the substances discussed in this section, nothing seems to be more mysterious and unexplained than the very nature of Dark Matter. What is it? Quite frankly, we have no idea. Not a single person has a single idea what it is but it makes up over 80 percent of the mass of the universe and can't, for some reason, be directly observed by any means available.

Though it can't be observed, by understanding the movements of stars, it was made obvious to researchers that there was a large amount of mass not accounted for. This mass would need to make up roughly 80 percent if it was to be able to hold the elements of the universe together, which is how scientists became aware of Dark Matter and its implications relative to the very nature of our universe. Understanding what it is, why it can't be detected and all of its strange properties could be the key to understanding big questions about the nature of our universe and existence in general. Until then, we will just have to sit and wonder what it is and why we can't exactly measure it in any way.

Superhuman Tribes
Around The World

All across the world are a variety of cultures, traditions, religions and people that create their own sense of community and growth as they develop within their social groups isolated from others. This sense of community and family stands out the most for tribesman that rely on not only each other for survival, but on the values and traditions they have held since their conception.

Of course, it isn't much of a mystery then that some of these tribes, isolated from the rest of the world, began on their own separate path from the general population and developed new ways to tackle difficult problems they and their tribesman faced. What is a mystery however, is that some of these developments, from isolated tribes from around the world, have baffled scientists and challenged what we used to believe was possible for humans to be able to accomplish. In this section, we will be going over five different tribes that are believed to have superhuman traits and how this is accomplished.

Number 1: The Kalenjin of Kenya

Referred to as "The Running Tribe", the people of the Kalenjin Tribe of Kenya occupy the majority of the Rift Valley in this region and make up an incredibly large population of almost five million people living in the area. These tribesmen come from an ancient line of people that originated in the valley and have been living in these ancient homelands since the Second Millennia B.C.. It is peculiar in most regard then that, despite issues where they predominantly reside relative to developments, necessary and healthy diets, physical activity and other environmental factors that can contribute to lack of nourishment, nutrition and standard of living, The Kalenjin Tribe of Kenya has such a tremendous advantage compared to the rest of the world in regards to athletic prowess.

Since the middle of the 1960's, the residents and population that arose from the Kalenjin Tribe of Kenya have won the largest collective share of major honors in international athletics from anywhere of distances between the 800 meter dash to that of the Marathon, making their tiny tribe the most decorated runners in the world for the categories of track and field. Involvement in competitions became more popular for the tribe from the 1980's and so on where, at about this time, the tribe had recieved a little more than 40 percent of the top honours available to men in all international athletics at the categories of track and field. This included competitions such as that of olympic medals, world championship medals, world cross country championship honors and many other international competitions.

Given these statistics and advancements, scientists and researchers have been puzzled as to the athletic prowess of the tribe and further research has shown that there are many factors that could be playing into their overall ability to perform consistently high level endurance and strength over great distances. It is also important to note that it is specifically people from this tribe that have the capability at performing consecutively at such a level as studies have found that others in the region that are not apart of the tribe do not possess the same abilities relative to athletic prowess.

Number 2: Bajau People of Indonesia

Referred to and commonly nicknamed the "Sea Nomads", the Bajau People of Indonesia live a complex seaborne life with their earliest traditions going back to the time of their native ancestors that used the area for its rich resources in the waters and lived the majority of their lives on the oceans. Even today there are still a vast amount of individuals within the tribe living their lives in small houseboats they refer to as Lepas and travel alongside other houseboats filled with their next of kin and immediate family.

Interestingly enough, this small tribe of approximately 1 million people has the incredible ability to spend the majority of their time underwater that greatly exceeds what scientists, researchers and health experts used to consider and believe was humanly possible. The Bajau People of Indonesia are world renowned for their advanced abilities in free diving and because of this can spend up to five hours per day underwater, on average. At a very early age the Bajau People will in- tentionally rupture their eardrums to be able to dive at greater depths to engage in long underwater searches and hunts. The true anomaly in their abilities, however, is the fact that the peo- ple of this remote tribe have the incredible ability of being able to hold their breath on average for a total of 13 minutes at a depth of 200 feet, roughly 20 stories deep.

For comparison with this statistic, the average person can only hold their breath for roughly 45 seconds to a minute, meaning that by the time you have surfaced for air 13 times, the Bajau People of Indonesia will only be coming back up for a quick breath. This is made all the more impressive at the depths they are able to hold their breath at, which for an average person could cut their breath holding capacity by half.

If you are wondering how this incredible feat is made possible, so are the researchers of whom have not yet been able to crack the code as to the tribe's ability to perform such an extraordinary act. A few scientists have found that after analyz- ing differences in the bodies of the tribesmen, that residents of the population have a spleen that is roughly 50 percent larger than the average population. Early theories as to the regulation of oxygen rich blood and the ability to hold their breath have been tied to this finding that has led researchers to believe that perhaps at greater depths after the spleen has contracted due to underwater pressures, it begins to expel oxygen-rich blood stored in the organ that allows continually underwater breathing for a prolonged period of time.

Number 3: The Sherpas Of The Himalayas

Located around the Himalayan mountains, the Sherpas are a tribe that originated from the native Nepalese and devel- oped special adaptations for their living conditions on the tallest and coldest mountains of the world. The Sherpas are regarded by even the most experienced mountain climbers as the elite experts in the world of hiking and mountain climbing and, due to this, are often hired on as guides or climbing supporters for mountaineering expeditions in the Himalayan region.

Interestingly enough, the Sherpas have developed unique

advantages in the world of mountain climbing and high altitude conditions. Not only do to their traditions allow them to learn advanced climbing techniques early on, but the Sherpas have special genetic adaptations to living at high altitudes that include richer oxygen levels in their blood and the ability to produce nitric oxide at double the normal rate of the average individual. Not only this, but given their long durations of being exposed to blistering weather and extremely cold conditions, the Sherpas have developed special brown fats that have a higher ability to generate natural heat in the body and prevent the cold from doing any lasting damaging effects to their bodies and to even prevent shivering in otherwise intolerable conditions.

Number 4: Native Ecuadorians With Laron Syndrome

One of the most radical and revolutionary discoveries of the modern century has to do with the genetic advancements and supposed super power of the native Ecuadorians that were born with the genetic defect of Laron Syndrome. After researchers began to notice a lack of cancer developments in the native Ecuadorian population among those with Laron Syndrome, a genetic defect that causes a form of dwarfism, they began looking into the anomaly with startling results.

For some unknown reason that, if better understood, could help us cure cancer in the modern era, research biologists have found that native Ecuadorians with Laron Syndrome have the supernatural ability to not develop cancers of any kind. In fact, when tests were attempted to form cancer causing cells in retrieved healthy cells of individuals of this population, they immediately began annihilating themselves rather than to grow and spread into tumors and replicating growths.

This ability is so valuable to the discovery of potential cures that a substantial amount of research efforts and genetic treatment analysis have been conducted relative to this population that could work to help save a tremendous amount of lives across the world and allow people to not have to worry about cancer related issues in the future.

Number 5: The Okinawan People of Japan

Probably the most interesting super power to be discussed today is a power that is held by the Okinawan People of Japan that have such an incredibly high statistic in regards to longevity that the average life expectancy of an Okinawan is far exceeding even in the neighboring people surrounding them, leading them to hold the title of the most long lived people on Earth.

The strangeness of this occurrence eludes even the most advanced attempts at researching this cause as there is no apparent evolutionary cause of this longevity and no advancements in genetic research relative to the Okinawans that help to shed any light on the matter. Though the incredibly long life-spans of the Okinawans is believed by scientists and research biologists to arise from genetic factors, the lack of any substantial findings leads researchers to believe the cause could be from a random genetic mutation and a combination of surrounding environmental factors.

It is found that the Okinawan People have several traditions that could boost the longevity of even normal individuals elsewhere in the world such as personal gardens that grow medicinal herbs of all varieties, an active lifestyle to help stay in shape, a lot of exposure to sun for a boost of Vitamin D, a reliance on a primarily plant-based diet and the embracement of a centuries old tradition called Ikigai that teaches the Okinawan people to live a purpose imbued life and to persevere through any obstacle thrown their way. There are many researchers who deny these environmental claims however as other Japanese populations follow these traditions and still do not have such high levels of longevity among their own populations.

Extraterrestrial

A Response Strategy
To Alien Invasions

It appears that every year there are new stories surfacing in the alien community that bring terrifying visions to mind. From sightings, to abductions, to recovered tracking devices and so on, the alarming rate of new alien experiences have led many to ask a very serious question. "Could it be possible that we are being studied for ulterior motives and a dangerous hidden agenda? Could this be the first step into an invasion tactic?"

In this section, we will be going over Project N.A.I.R., a four step plan that helps to illustrate, in an accurate measure, the most appropriate steps taken by humankind in the event of an alien invasion. The Project stands for Negotiations, Annihilation, Investigation, and Retaliation. So, in the article below, we will be going over, in fine detail, what humans would do if there was an alien invasion.

Step One: Negotiations

As aliens approach our planet, it would be incredibly important for the countries of our world to begin the processes of taking the necessary preparations required to create an open dialogue between ourselves and the extraterrestrial visitors. Even if aliens have the full intention of attacking our planet, there is a vital reason as to why they would postpone this attack and open up a means of communication with human beings prior to this event.

Information.

It is most likely safe to assume that life is quite unique in the universe. Given this fact, it is also safe to assume that if a species had the ability to travel a great distance across time and space to get to the human race, then it is significantly more advanced than us in any way. This ultimately means that problems such as the need for resources and so on would not be relevant for their societies. With this known, it would be crucial to open up a dialogue to engage discussions about the importance of trading information. If life is unique, then automatic destruction would not be viable and it would work in the favor of the extraterrestrials and ourselves to first trade scientific information as if it was currency.

This will help us to slowly negotiate to understand their weapons and technologies while providing vital information gathered relative to DNA, studies, inventions and other pieces of information that would not have been available to them on their home planet.

These negotiations could then buy us some time to analyze further information and better understand our potential enemy before any shots had been fired and so would be incredibly crucial for us to engage in. This could also help to meet a temporary peace agreement with outlining territories, trades, rules and regulations and so on that could help to establish a lasting dialogue and prevent a full out war altogether.

Step Two: Annihilation

Either negotiations have failed or the extraterrestrials have gathered all the information they feel is important regarding the human species and have now begun enacting their plans of destruction. Depending on their technology and the technological evolution of their weaponry, this attack could take years, months, weeks, days or maybe even hours.

The attack would most likely be swift, strategic and unexpected. They would begin their attack by first deactivating or destroying the satellites surrounding the planet in the attempt to cut off large scale communications and imaging. After this first step had been completed, they would then begin targeting areas with a high density of populations such as major cities with quick demolishing blasts or invasion tactics. This will help to maximise their damage and impact while simultaneously taking out a hub of important production zones, power grids, cell towers and communications.

This was to be expected, with such an overbearing power, human beings were always at the mercy of the alien visitors. Thanks to the negotiations step, however, information would have been traded to help provide insight as to possible weapons used and ways to counteract them. Most conventional and unconventional weapons can be stopped by simply going underground and using the Earth as a natural barrier against kinetic weapons, radiation, laser technology or biochemical warfare. During the first step, the building of these safe zones would have been crucial and would allow a significant portion of human beings to survive the initial attack.

In a strange silver-lining, the attack would also help to unite the human race against a common enemy. A similar situation was seen amongst the Ancient Greek cities states that spend eons battling against each other but united upon learning of the invading powerful Persian forces. With preparations for this attack and surviving the initial incoming destruction, the event itself will be fuel to unite all the surviving countries, nations, forces and ideologies into one unified army against our extraterrestrial invaders.

Step Three: Investigations

When the majority of the attack has finished, it would be incredibly important for human beings to begin investigating and assessing the situation. How many people were lost? What strategies did the aliens use? How many countries and governments are still operating, if any? But most importantly, what weapons did the aliens use?

Understanding and attempting to reverse engineer the weapons aliens have used will allow us to understand how to damage them. Of course, weapons are made with the intention of destroying neighboring countries and nations. This would mean that any weapons the aliens have made would have the capability of damaging themselves as in-fighting and civil war is common in all species.

By investigating the damages, the tactics, the weapons and so on, human beings could then begin gathering further information and coming up with a viable solution to retaliate. Though they may be advanced, human beings know war better than anyone else. During this point in time when the first wave of attacks have subsided and the extraterrestrial forces are preparing for further attacks, human beings would be granted a window of opportunity to conduct this investigation period to better use existing technology, any surviving forces and any surviving countries and orchestrate an attack plan in secret. This would rely on key information gathered so it could very well be that the most important step of this entire plan relies solely on time management, resources and expertise in investigations.

Step Four: Retaliation

The information has been gathered, armies have been instructed and human beings are pushing back with every last breath they have. Retaliation works to orchestrate a complex plan that must be completed as quickly as possible and with the hope of ending a fight before it continues any longer. The longer a retaliating attack takes, the less advantage is provided with such an attack and may only lead to extraterrestrial forces locating further survivors and finishing out their initial attack.

Using information gathered during the investigation phase, humans would be able to understand key weaknesses and strengths in the alien forces and their technology. This would allow a one-time retaliating attack that must be completed in as little time as possible with the focus of ending the fight before it can begin. It is of utmost importance that as little time is given for extraterrestrial forces to understand and prepare. If a vital weakness is made apparent, they may very well possess the ability to adapt and change this weakness faster than an attack can be held out.

It is also incredibly important to note that we would not be given the luxury of holding anything back. There is no room for future diplomacy and there is no room for a second chance. The retaliating attack is the end-all attack to any further tactics. There is no room for error or for future plans. Any attempts at dialogue would also have to be completely prevented as this can be used by an extraterrestrial force to track or analyze further information or be made aware of the retaliating attack further.

By utilizing every nation's forces in a single all-out attack, there are some advantages and disadvantages. If everything is delivered and no further ammunition and weapons are available then it could very well mean that we would be leaving ourselves wide open if the retaliating attack did not work, but that should not be of much concern considering the fact that if the retaliating attack fails anyway then the last of the human beings would not be sticking around long enough to make another.

Are Aliens Interested In Nuclear Weapons?

Though many people would argue that the existence of extraterrestrial life is implausible, there are numerous government officials and nuclear guardians at United States Missile silos that would beg to differ and have worked to challenge the modern understanding of extraterrestrial life and their involvement in the United States military. In 1966, Nuclear Missile Officer and Nuclear Guardian, of whom had worked at an undisclosed United States Air Force Nuclear Silo, named Robert Salas, claimed that the nuclear missiles stored at these silos, of which were ready to fire, were suddenly shut off by an unidentified flying object hovering over the United States Air Force Base.

Mr. Robert Salas is reported as saying *"Our missiles began going into what's called a no-go condition or unlaunchable. Essentially, they were disabled."* further details of the accounts can be found in an undisclosed report titled Affidavit of Charles I. Halt of which is filled not with just the witness testimony of Mr. Robert Salas but with detailed court sanctioned sworn affidavits including other witness testimonies from Nuclear Guardians, politicians, high positioned military officers and research scientists from numerous nuclear missile silos and various locations.

As ridiculous as this might seem to most, the accounts were so detailed and gathered proof of the unidentified craft continued throughout the 1960's so extensively that the now disclosed project was a major concern for the United States National Security during its heightened claims of UFO involvement.

Now spearheaded by a ufo researcher named Robert Hastings, additional reports of these unidentified craft and nuclear involvement have been surfacing from around the world. Mr Hastings gave a speech at Washington D.C. that had broadcasted his findings and claims across the world that read as the following:

"The witnesses have described these craft as 'disc-shaped' or cylindrical shaped, or spherical... In 1966 according to a launch officer, David Shore, his missiles were temporarily activated just as his security guard was reporting a bright object moving from missile to missile to missile..."

Mr. Robert Hastings' speech was not concerned with the proof of extraterrestrial life nor the political and scientific implications of the findings. His number one concern was surrounding one issue and one issue only. National security. His investigation wasn't originally focused around UFO involvement but found this to be the only plausible explanation as he continued in his speech where he detailed similar incidents he had uncovered in his investigations in then Soviet Ukraine.

"Given the fact that these incidents that have gone on over there, including one incident of their missiles being temporarily activated when a UFO was hovering above the missile base, identical to what occurred here, I think we can rule out that whoever are piloting these craft are American or Russian."

Interestingly enough, these were not the only cases that UFO researchers have found on claims of alien involvement with nuclear missile bases as the research provided details of decades of involvement and incidents relative to unidentified flying objects at many other nuclear missile bases as well.

If you believe that the information being told here sounds implausible, you can find these reports online, watch news clips that exist and conduct your own research into legitimate military documents and investigations concerning the United States and Russian national security issues.

Given the evidence and the research that has been provided, could it be true that aliens are trying to prevent us from nuking our planet and killing ourselves? Of course, from a purely scientific perspective, if we assume their intentions to be legitimate, they could be working around the clock to prevent such actions as a nuclear holocaust in the hopes of studying us further and assisting our evolution into an intergalactic species similar to themselves.

However, as someone who conducts research and works to have a skeptical mind, pure intentions are ever hardly the case in the world of politics. In fact, aliens could be working behind the scenes in a secret agenda, influencing our nuclear weapons, pressuring our politicians and attempting to accomplish a goal of their own selfish choosing.

Could their involvement with our nuclear weapons be

rather an attempt at them displaying power, or even hoping to prevent us from killing ourselves so that they may continue to manipulate us and control us from the shadows?

A huge piece of evidence to consider is that though there are incidents of these unidentified flying objects disabling nuclear devices, there are a tremendous amount of more incidents in the reports of these disc-shaped crafts attempting to activate our nuclear arsenal and lead us into a full on nuclear strike.

In fact, the greatest piece of evidence for this involvement with nuclear politics could be a secret cover up made recently that the general public has been attempting to ignore.

On January 13th of 2018, across the state of Hawaii there was a nuclear scare so frightening and real, it lead to an overall mind shift in the general population of the United States and its citizens. The threats of a potential nuclear holocaust became a reality. The American population held their breaths as they realized the fears no one treated seriously were very much at their doorsteps as the entire population of Hawaii was sent the following message on their phone from the emergency alerts system.

"*Ballistic Missile threat inbound to Hawaii. Seek immediate shelter. This is not a drill.*"

It had appeared that the situation involving the nuclear advancements of North Korea had reached their climax and that these intercontinental ballistics missiles were soon on their way to deliver their final load; However, exactly 38 minutes later, a second message was sent to the entire population of Hawaii. It read the following.

"*False Alarm.*"

38 minutes.

Exactly the amount of time it takes for an ICBM launched from North Korea to strike U.S. soil. In fact, leaked Central Intelligence Agency documents gave reported intelligence that the North Korean Nuclear missiles had the capacity to reach United States soils but only as far as Hawaii. A strange coincidence that the only state to have issued the nuclear scare is the only state that would have been threatened by the North Korean nuclear missile advancements.

Immediately after this supposed false alarm, North Korea and South Korea, thought to have never happen in our generation, signed a peace treaty agreement and have been working together to overcome the differences and conditions of the opposing neighboring nations.

What if then, the history we are told is incredibly false?

Let us posit a question. What if there was a nuclear missile strike and what if the United States backed off with its political involvement after these very real threats were made. Donald Trump continually talked about North Korea before this point and even gave detailed instructions that North Korean officials were bluffing. This all fell silent after this incident in Hawaii.

What if then, there really was a nuke sent to Hawaii and instead of hitting Hawaii, someone stopped it and, to cover up this scare, the United States issued a false alarm? There is no technology in the world that has the ability to stop a nuclear strike. In fact, the United States military had been attempting to work on these technologies but failed continually as they attempted to better understand a way to prevent a sudden nuclear attack.

Described by research scientists as "Stopping a bullet with another bullet", it was deemed highly unlikely to the point of statistical impossibility. Yet perhaps, there is a technology that can stop nuclear missiles, a technology that no human possesses, a technology created and controlled by extraterrestrial life.

Further evidence is given as the months following this incident has shown Russian research into nuclear missiles that cannot be intercepted, almost as if the country believes that the United States possesses technology to prevent a nuclear strike.

In March of 2018, two months after the Hawaii incident, Vladimir Putin, the current Russian president, gave a detailed speech talking about Russian nuclear missiles and their advancements into unstoppable interceptions. Could this have been because Russia believes the United States military had intercepted the North Korean Ballistics missiles?

In our theory, we have established timing, evidence and conspiracy. So how does it all tie together? What if Aliens were focused on creating peace amongst the North Korean and South Korean nations and helped to stop the nuclear missiles from striking the United States and leading to a full on nuclear holocaust around the world.

What many people don't understand is that the United States and other countries that contain a nuclear arsenal, have a mathematical philosophy in place called Mutually Assured Destruction, referred to as M.A.D.

If you think you're safe, you're not. Mutually Assured Destruction works to prevent any nation from using nukes by having automatic nuclear retaliation in the event of a nuke being fired. These nukes wouldn't just be targeted at the enemy, they would be targeted everywhere. If we die, you die. We all die. This philosophy works to prevent any single nation risking the lives of the human race and working to never use such technological destruction.

Could it have been then that a secret alien race worked to influence the politics of the world by interfering with nuclear politics and military strikes? We have detailed evidence of alien involvement at nuclear missile silos with the ability to activate and deactivate Intercontinental ballistic missiles carrying nuclear payloads.

I am not here stating that this is the case or that we have definitive proof on the matter, I am merely positing forward questions and evidence uncovered that could help to provide us a picture of the nonsensical happenings of our modern history and political shifts.

Are Aliens Reading Our Thoughts?

A trend that is seen across popular science fiction movies are numerous depictions of aliens that have the ability to telepathically communicate with an outside species or amongst themselves. This has been a long held belief of UFO and alien experts and has been witnessed time and time again by abductees and the accounts they detail during their abductions and their containment as they were being studied and tested by extraterrestrial life.

Claims of supposed instances of telepathy can vary from seeing detailed images in their mind that appear to be symbols, mathematical expressions, complex images, hearing a voice inside their head and even being unable to discern their own thoughts with the thoughts being planted into their minds to control them and hypnotize them by the alien life they encounter.

Given the scientific evidence and developments of the human brain today, is there a way to explain this phenomenon and give credence to the idea that aliens could be reading our minds and planting foreign thoughts?

Before we continue further into these claims, it is important to note that there is evidence and scientific endeavors in the realm of Neuroscience and the ability to translate the neuron's near-random electrical impulse firings into readable information that can be displayed or understood. In fact, back in 1999, there was a research study by Dan Yang at the University of Berkeley California that successfully recreated what a cat observes in the physical world using pure data retrieved from visual neurons.

So, how can we retrieve data from neurons and how does this help us? Though many might not believe it and still regard such sciences as within the realm of the supernatural, that is hardly the case. Using an E.E.G. machine, one can gather information from the brain using a Differential Amplifier that merely works to gather data from two electrical inputs and measures the difference compared against each other in electrical occurrence and shows that data as an output. That means that data can be retrieved from the brain by merely detecting the electrical impulses through the scalp of a human being and comparing it to other regions of the brain as a whole.

The implications of this finding means that if someone could create a technology so sensitive and accurate in picking up electromagnetic fields or electrical stimuli, one could remotely detect these occurrences coming from the human brain and work to gather the data required to translate your thoughts and brain signals into readable information.

But that does not help to explain the strange phenomenon that occurs in supposed alien contacts via telepathic communications. If such a device is used then how is it that humans, when exposed to extraterrestrial life, have the ability to communicate telepathically back to said alien contacts and why is there no mention of the appearance of such a device?

It could very well be that aliens evolved this ability to communicate telepathically through natural means in their evolutionary pathways. All life will evolve some ability and means to communicate with their own kind in some various method and not all methods include vocalizations like human communications. Some forms of life use smells, physical contact, body language and so on, so is it within the realm of possibility for telepathic communication to have occured for intellectually advanced forms of life?

Let us treat this as a thought experiment. As you advance technologically, war and technologies could become incredibly dangerous and lead to self-annihilation if these routes continue and a lasting peace can not be established. However, a great way to avoid conflict is to establish a means of open communication and work to better understand the situation at hand. Have you ever tried to communicate a thought but found words to be a terrible delivery method of translating emotions, personal experiences, observations and context? What if all life that develops methods of communications that are not able to more accurately represent their inner monologues also lose the ability to equally grow their intelligence as a species? Or in this sense, annihilate themselves before becoming an intergalactic race? Could it be then that an intergalactic species would have to naturally form telepathic communications with one another evolutionarily to prevent such catastrophes and to be able to advance so far technologically?

Is there evidence of animals on earth that might be able to evolve in this manner?

If we take this theory of data retrieval from the brains of animals via sensing electrical impulses and changes in the electromagnetic field, then there is evidence of evolution granting this ability amongst life here on Earth. Referred to as electroreception, it is a sense that humans do not seem to possess that gives animals the ability to perceive natural electrical stimuli in other forms of life around them. Electroreception, on Earth, has only been seen to occur almost exclusively in aquatic life or amphibious animals that spend their time in salt water since salt water is a much better natural conductor compared to surrounding air. This ability is so sensitive, in fact, that young sharks can recognize the specific characteristics and traits of electrical stimuli amongst predators and hide before the creature even comes within sight.

Now you might be thinking that if this ability can only occur underwater, then how does that help our theory? This is actually not the case, there are exceptions in electroreception of species communicating via electrical stimuli outside of water as well. The currently known exceptions are monotremes, cockroaches and bees.

Could this be evidence of life on our very own planet naturally developing methods in evolution that allow for non-verbal communication via electrical signals and readings through telepathy alone?

Another interesting development in UFO and alien researchers is the lack of verbal communication from extraterrestrial contacts. There are no reports of a screaming, screeching, yelling or vocalization of any kind coming from supposed alien abduction reports or alien encounters. What is even more alerting to this strange phenomenon is the continually self-consistent reports of telepathic communication in nearly all witness accounts concerning communications with extraterrestrial life. Could this be a statistical reference of their inability to communicate verbally and only telepathically?

If we then can prove theoretically that aliens could evolve the natural ability to read our minds telepathically, then how can we explain an aliens ability to speak to us if we do not naturally have the ability to read their minds? This could still be very easily explained evolutionarily.

If our brains transfer information via electrical signals, one could theoretically then stimulate certain areas of our brain using electricity to create new memories, experiences or transfer data. This has already been accomplished in the realm of modern science with the creation of the God Helmet that works to enhance areas of the brain that are responsible with areas of religious experience and can stimulate the mind in such a way to create vast hallucinations and images in your mind.

There are numerous well-known species across the Earth that have an ability to some degree to manipulate electrical signals of the body. The Eel, in fact, can deliver voltage that can paralyze or stun their predators allowing them to get away with ease. In essence, if extraterrestrial life developed a means of sending precise electrical information biologically, they would be able to develop a direct means of communication with nearly all life in the universe.

This does imply, however, that alien life could very well possess the ability to control you with their mind by hijacking your brain or planting their own thoughts that may be confused with your own thoughts. This does mean that any form of telepathic communication with said extraterrestrial life could be a dangerous means of risking subtle influences of your own body and mind. It would then be imperative and of utter importance to minimize means of telepathic communication and to rather make attempts at preventing such invasions of the brain.

Conspiracy theorists would point to tinfoil hats as a main precaution against extraterrestrial life, but the information surrounding electric stimulation proves that a tinfoil hat could actually work to enhance your brainwaves and possibly make it easier for extraterrestrial life to conduct telepathic communications.

If our previous assumptions and theories hold true relative to the mechanisms of telepathic communications and their developments, then the only way to prevent unwanted mental intrusions would be to create a portable Faraday Cage that could work to accurately block any incoming electrical signals or electromagnetic fields while simultaneously preventing your own mind from emitting electrical stimuli. Of course, a Faraday Cage would prove to be rather heavy and annoying to move around inside, so a more practical technology would need to be used if wanting to engage in contact and to not be limited to the confines of a cage.

Luckily enough, there are such developments. Using advancements in electromagnetic shielding garments, one could create an entire working Faraday Suit that could work similar to a Faraday Cage and to protect oneself from supposed mental attacks via telepathic communications. In fact, such suits are already on the market and can be purchased by the general public as most of these garments are worn to protect workers from strong electromagnetic fields and powerlines.

Wearing such a suit would completely prevent telepathic communication, and thusly an invasion of the mind, while also providing mobility and comfortability that a normal Faraday Cage could not provide.

But of course, that requires our previous assumptions and theories relative to telepathic communication to be true and given the lack of scientific evidence and testing, we are merely working off an educated guess and practical application of theory.

Does The Sphinx Predate The Egyptians?

When the Ancient Greek civilization first journeyed to Egypt and laid witness to its incredible methods of construction, megalithic structures, advanced cities and technologies along with the civilization's incredible strides in mathematics and philosophy, not only were they completely intrigued by this, but they quickly worked to try to classify what they saw and provided it with the names we know today. When the Ancient Greeks came across the large stone structure that depicted a lion with the face of a man, reminding the Greeks of the stories of the Sphinx recorded in the struggle of Oedipus, they quickly named the structure the Sphinx as an ode to their own culture seen in the Egyptian culture; however, outside of this original encounter, nothing else was known about the strange structure.

In fact, new evidence and research today has found that it could very well be possible that the Sphinx structure itself is far older than supposed Egyptian writings and documents proclaim it to be. In this section, we will be going over this evidence regarding the Sphinx and asking ourselves the question: Does the Great Sphinx of Egypt pre-date the Egyptian civilization itself?

One of the main reasons for why the Sphinx has been dated its current age of being only 4,511 years old is not due to carbon dating or other reliable efforts made to accurately measure its date but rather because of Ancient Egyptian Hieroglyphics and documents that detail that the Sphinx was supposedly created during the reign of Egypt's Fourth Dynasty. Unfortunately, it was recently discovered that these documents could very well not be legitimate and that the Pharaoh of the Fourth Dynasty forged them for the sole purpose of taking credit of another past pharaoh's works, a common practice amongst pharaohs to rewrite history and take the honor of a past pharaoh's life long efforts. This was discovered not by taking a closer inspection at the Sphinx, but rather, discoveries made in the tombs of long deceased Kings of Egypt.

Originally a theory posited by the groundbreaking author Robert Temple, there appeared to be overwhelming evidence that the Sphinx we know today was actually an attempt made by a pharaoh of the Fourth dynasty to do nothing more than to claim the works of those before him. Evidence for this can be found when analyzing the head-to-body ratio of the large statue. The head on the Sphinx is so small that many had often believed, upon first sight, that it could have been grinded down from a much more massive structure. The second piece of evidence is provided by the Hieroglyphics located at the Temple of Tep-Tu-F (Tehp-Too-Fuh) that outline in great detail that the original God of Ancient Giza was Anubis and the accounts and images of Anubis in his jackal form are drawn all throughout the site in the same pose as of the body of the Sphinx with no mention of a lion of any kind at the ancient city.

Interestingly enough this exact same pose was discovered in one of the only tombs of an Egyptian pharaoh ever discovered that had been completely undisturbed since his burial, the tomb of Pharaoh Tutankhamun. Within King Tut's tomb is a shrine to Anubis that demonstrates an exact scale of the Sphinx statue but with the head of a jackal to represent Anubis, showing in overwhelming evidence that the original statue at the Ancient City of Giza was supposed to be that of a jackal-headed Anubis and not that of a lion body with a human head. So, where do we get the idea of a human head and a lion body?

The truth is, the only reason why the statue is referred to as a Sphinx is because of old Greek mythologies, such as those of Oedipus, that talk about a lion with the head of a man called a Sphinx but no such symbol exists in that of Ancient Egypt. This means that the Hieroglyphic texts that describe the Sphinx with a human head to represent the Pharaoh of the Fourth Dynasty were nothing more than forgeries by the then pharoah to take credit for a great statue of which he had not created nor designed.

In fact, a Predynastic Pharaoh gives a great account about providing his royal dog a grand burial at the site of Ancient Giza. In this text, his argument for why he had such a royal burial for what has been speculated to be his guard dog was due to his want and need to have the dog buried before the great God Anubis. Not only definitively proving that the Sphinx was originally that of the God Anubis in the jackal form but also that the structure itself was created during the predynastic times long before any pharaoh could claim ownership of its creation.

This could very well mean that not only was the creation of the Sphinx older than that of the dynastic reigns of Egypt, but that perhaps the structure is older than the Egyptian civilizations themselves. Further evidence of this theory can be found when analyzing the recent archaeological finds of strange bones discovered all throughout Ancient Egypt. It is well known amongst Egyptologists that the Ancient Egyptians treasured animals of all kinds, believing them to be the representation of their Gods. It is due to this obsession that strange structures and bones from animals all around the world, even from areas previously believed to not have been operating open trade routes, have surfaced all across Ancient Egyptian cities. Described as Egyptian zoos, strange Hieroglyphics and designs have come forward showing evidence that not only were the early Egyptians capable of owning strange beasts from around the world but that they possibly possessed an extinct species of Wooly Mammoth.

Dubbed as the world's first zoo, a 6,000 year old Ancient Egyptian cemetery was uncovered filled with the remains of wild animals from all around the world that should have been unable to collect from the reaches of early man for thousands of years to come. Skeletons of ostriches, crocodiles, leopards and other exotic animals were found alongside pools of water, large fenced-in cages and a potential animal hospital filled with removed molars, teeth, claws and evidence of animal surgeries. Though the importance of animals regarding the Egyptian religion was widely known, the evidence of the global reach of the species available to them, including species long believed to be extinct, has been a mystery that even the most elite of Archeologists and Egyptologists have failed to explain.

This is odd though mostly due to the fact that it is widely believed by Historians and Archaeologists all around the world that the oldest civilization to exist was merely 10,000 years old; however, evidence in the fossil record shows that the modern day intelligent human has been around for more than 50,000 years. If this is true, why is it then that the oldest cities don't start appearing until the past 10,000? It might have to do with the evidence of the extinct animals recorded at Egypt.

The Wooly Mammoth was one of many distinct megafauna that went extinct at around the same time in the fossil record, merely 10,000 years ago. These extinct species included the Mastodon, Short-faced bear, the giant Ground Sloth and many others. In fact, when Charles Darwin first visited the areas near the Galapagos Island, when he originally discovered the Ground Sloth bones, they were so fresh that he believed them to be a still living species of megafauna, ultimately proving the recency of their extinction. So why was it then that around 10,000 years ago all of these species went extinct? Partly due to three strange reasons, large fires, a massive flood and a sudden ice age.

The evidence for these three events are widely known by Archaeologists and research scientists that found in the fossil record evidence that showed that, all around the Earth, there appeared to be massive fires that were followed by a rapid cooling event that only took about four decades as well as certain events being hit by numerous tsunamis and large flooding. Many experts had originally speculated that perhaps a massive meteorite strike could have caused such a phenomenon but no large craters supporting the theory had yet been discovered at the time of the original publications.

However, recently, a massive crater underneath an ice sheet in Greenland shows a tremendous impact point where a meteor could have hit, generating more than 700 megatons of force. So much force in fact that it would have been equivalent to 140 fully efficient nuclear strikes using the Tsar Bomba nuclear warhead, a nuke capable of not only breaking the Stratosphere but generating enough dust and debris in the air to cause a full on nuclear winter.
Any human civilization at the time, regardless of how advanced, would have been completely wiped off the face of the Earth in such a massive meteor strike. All of this happening at not only around the same time as a massive extinction event but also around the same time the oldest civilizations would have been constructed.

Could this be evidence then that perhaps the Pyramids at Giza and the Sphinx as well as many other advancements made in megalithic structures and creations could actually more accurately have come from the efforts of human beings from before this catastrophic event and the Egyptians were merely one of many surviving people to pick up where humanity left off? Given the incredible advancements we have made in the past 10,000 years, this could very well mean that the humans before the event could have been significantly more advanced than we are today and the old stories of gods and kings could very well have just been the technological advancements before humanity had to reset due to such a catastrophic tragedy.

Or even more frightening, could these structures have been created by life and advanced civilizations that originate from outside of our planet? Perhaps these structures are evidence of a far more advanced race that had spent its time cultivating and constructing on our planet, of whom were forced to leave or become eradicated by a cataclysmic event not too long ago in our planet's history.

Evidence Of The Extraterrestrial Threat

One of the most overwhelming pieces of evidence in relation to the issue of national security regarding the story of extraterrestrial life is that of an alien known as Val Valiant Thor. Though many skeptics widely regard the existence of extraterrestrials as being an incredible impossibility, not only is there overwhelming evidence of extraterrestrial life having visited our pale blue planet but that this life infiltrated the highest levels of government and manipulated high military intelligence officials before finishing its mission and leaving the planet with gathered military intelligence. The name of this extraterrestrial was that of Val Valiant Thor and according to the evidence recovered, it is merely one of many others that have used the same tactics and strategies to infiltrate different levels of government security. Proving the issue of extraterrestrials to be that of national security concerns and overwhelming threat of outside life.

Back in 1967, the extraterrestrial community became aware of the book titled "Stranger at the Pentagon" that detailed information regarding a possible extraterrestrial visitor that worked alongside military intelligence officials at the Pentagon in the United States. Though many believed that perhaps the book was nothing more than a hoax, recent news has surfaced about the legitimacy of the book when it was authenticated by the whistleblower Phil Schnieder of whom not only agreed that the book was a factual description of the events regarding the Pentagon but that the extraterrestrial known as Val Valiant Thor worked alongside his father.

In fact, Phil Schnieder went on record and claimed that he had a picture of Val Valiant Thor and showed it to many different people at his lecture taken back in August of 1943 with irrefutable proof of the location being taken at a high military intelligence official location. Unfortunately, before further copies of the image could be created, Phil Schnieder had been found dead shortly thereafter, making the last video recording of Phil Schnieder the only evidence of his claims and the picture he possessed of which can be found on YouTube today. Due to this, Phil Schnieder's passing makes the last video clip recorded and the book "Stranger at the Pentagon" the only surviving witness account of the events.

According to the book, Val Valiant Thor landed on March 16th, 1957, in Alexandria, Virginia, where two policemen approached the craft with their weapons drawn on the alien only for him to immediately counter their attacks by using advanced techniques of what was described as "thought transference" to essentially use mind control to manipulate the policemen to drop their weapons and drive him to Washington D.C., which is exactly what they did without any hesitation or struggle. This would not be the last of the extent of this mind control tactic used as Val Valiant Thor would then go on to manipulate high military personnel that allowed him to pass through high security posts to reach the Pentagon and then, furthermore, the White House itself to be granted an audience with the then United States President, Dwight D. Eisenhower. This is where the alien's dishonesty would shine and the clear statement of his intentions would come through.

Val Valiant Thor made the incredible claim to the United States president that his mission was to come to the planet Earth and provide a means to not only grant free energy for all of the Earth's residents but to usher in a new golden age that worked to solve all illnesses, deformities, crippling conditions and so on, though never described an accurate definition as to what he perceived as illnesses and crippling conditions. Though many supporters of Val Valiant Thor himself believe this to be a genuine want and proposition, there appears to be overwhelming evidence for the contrary. In fact, it appears to be obvious that the intentions of Val Valiant Thor were far more sinister than expected.

The striking noticeability of these sinister means was his blatant disregard for the rights to free will. All throughout the book and various witness accounts, it talks about how Val Valiant Thor used strange techniques in telepathy and mind control to gain access to high military intelligence or to trick individuals into helping him for a various amount of tasks and access points. These strange mental tricks included making people act as a slave to his will, causing people to see odd and vivid hallucinations of all different kinds, as well as convincing complete strangers to trust him and become attracted to him as he gave lectures at random alien and UFO meetups across Virginia and

Washington D.C.

These tricks and miracles would only become more and more horrifying in their nature as the true mission of Val Valiant Thor came to light. Even though the extraterrestrial visitor was a self-proclaimed savior of humanity, supposedly wanting nothing more than to provide a vaguely advanced technology capable of curing all disease and illnesses as well as providing free energy, next to no effort was provided into completing this mission. In fact, when Val Valiant Thor approached the President of the United States and came forward with this proposition, Dwight D. Eisenhower said that it could very well cause a danger to the industries of Capitalism and to humanity in general if there were no struggles left to overcome.

The President claimed that obstacles and pain are the driving forces of human nature and if a supposed peace on Earth were to exist, humanity would slowly devolve into nothing and no great minds could prosper and solve issues if no issues existed. Essentially clarifying that if all of our help came from an extraterrestrial force, humanity would be forced into a premature state of infancy relying solely on extraterrestrial technology and become an inherent slave race of these forces. After hearing this, Val Valiant Thor completely redacted his efforts to provide these technologies and seemed almost perfectly content with not helping humanity. In fact, the whole proposition turned out to be nothing more than an obvious bluff.

Shortly after this, Val Valiant Thor then began to try to convince the United States President if it could take him aboard its spaceship and take him back to its home planet of Venus. Eisenhower then asked Val Valiant Thor where his home planet was specifically and what it was like. Val Valiant Thor then replied that his homeplanet was the planet Venus, the second planet from the Sun, and that it was a paradise on Earth with beautiful lush green forests and heavenly atmospheres.

Of course, at this time, no one was aware of what the surface of Venus looked like, and though the planet was known to have a lot of the same characteristics as Earth, nothing else more was understood. The truth is known today that the surface of Venus is a blazing hot planet of which is more hell-like in its appearance than anything Val Valiant Thor claimed for it to be, marking one of the first and obvious dishonest statements he would provide. Luckily, the President had the sense to refuse and instead had the extraterrestrial detained at the headquarters of the Department of Defense known as the Pentagon.

This move turned out to be exactly what the extraterrestrial visitor was hoping for; however, as Val Valiant Thor allowed many to believe he was contained within the Pentagon but many other witness reports discussed personnel seeing Val Valiant Thor roaming around the area without supervision and accessing secret military intelligence files. It was believed that Val Valiant Thor was using a nearly supernatural ability as many of these witness reports regarded seeing the alien in an ethereal form wandering around but that when they would enter the room of which it was supposedly staying in, it would be there acting as if nothing was going on. Shortly after these stunts, it became apparent that the alien could not be completely contained and that he was perhaps acting as a spy to gather intelligence information for extraterrestrial forces.

These tensions reached a climax after the Department of Defense began doing state-of-the-art testing against the clothing materials brought by Val Valiant Thor itself. The materials were described as being completely indestructible in nature. When Val Valiant Thor became aware of these tests, it merely snickered and explained that humans were not capable of causing any damage to its clothes or to itself and seemingly laughed off the idea of being stopped. Threatened by this, the United States general conducting the investigations confronted Val Valiant Thor. Seemingly immune to its attempts at mind control, the general made a few key observations.

The general brought up the fact that it seemed more than a little peculiar that Val Valiant Thor would make his appearance only after the invention and use of the nuclear weapon. The general then clarified that even though modern weapons were incapable of damaging the clothes and the extraterrestrial himself, he more than was aware of how an atom bomb works and how it not only annihilates all matter but that, due to the neutrino bombardment, atoms themselves are split apart. Essentially, these comments made by the general were threatening the alien that if a weapon can't hurt him, an atom bomb surely could.

The general then made the rather brilliant connection that it appeared to him that extraterrestrials were only now getting involved as a ploy to gather military intelligence due to their fear of humanity's ability to now stand a chance in a fight. Val Valiant Thor then confirmed his sinister orders by not only clarifying that there were other extraterrestrial beings already infiltrating the United States, a supposed 77 others in fact, but that even more were walking amongst the human race all across the world. A number that would only continue to grow in the coming years. Not only does this whole-heartedly prove the extraterrestrial intention against the human race but that the threat of these alien visitors as a national security safety concern is overwhelming in nature.

Proof Advanced Civilizations Existed

Strange archaeological discoveries surrounding out-of-place artifacts come from all around the world at many different times in human history. Interestingly enough, despite the incredible evidence behind these finds, if an artifact is found to not fit within the expected timeline or supposed theories, it is quite usually dismissed entirely by the archaeological community and rejected by mainstream experts. Unfortunately, this mentality leads many down a rabbit hole of misinformation. In this section, we will be discussing these out-of-place artifacts and how they could prove the viability of ancient and advanced civilizations.

Number 1: The London Hammer

Also known by the name of the London Artifact, the London hammer was discovered in London, Texas, in 1936 and appears to be a hammer made entirely of iron and wood that was encased in a 400 million year old rock. Due to this embedded concretion, the object is widely regarded as an anomalous artifact of which has led many archaeologists and experts asking themselves how an obviously man-made tool could come to be encased in a 400 million year old rock.

Interestingly enough, further tests of the metal hammerhead suggests that the tool was used for craft specialization and was involved in fine work for softer metals. Even more strange is the fact that, even though the hammer head is made out of more than 96 percent iron, the artifact has not rusted a single speck since its discovery in the mid 1930's, leading some to believe that not only does the hammer contain a possible strange alloy but that it might have exceptionally advanced protection allowing for it to have been preserved for an incredibly long time. This has led many in the time travel conspiracy groups to argue that not only is this hammer evidence of time travel but that humans of the future could have been assisting the humans of the past and delivering advanced technologies for the creation of early civilizations.

Number 2: The Quimbaya Airplanes

Seen on many popular television shows such as that of the Ancient Aliens T.V. Show on the History Channel, as well as the Chariots of the Gods special, the Quimbaya Airplanes have been a massive symbol used by Ancient Astronaut theorists of whom argue that not only were advanced technologies available during these ancient times but that findings of these old technologies can be replicated today as both evidence and definitive proof of advanced Ancient civilizations. The Quimbaya Airplanes are a collection of several dozen golden objects apart of the Quimbaya artifacts found in Colombia. The artifacts were created by the Quimbaya civilization dated around 1,000 BCE and feature intricate designs that look suspiciously like airplanes.

The artifact shows a clear vertical rudder, back wing flaps, a cockpit, cigar-like body and depictions of winds traveling over the wings similarly seen in aerodynamics testings of the airfoil of aerodynamics and the wind traveling over the wings of a modern airplane. Due to its out of place nature, many archaeologists disregarded the find as nothing more than that of a symbolic object incapable of being a depiction of flight; however, in 1994, Peter Belting and Conrad Lubbers, two german engineers, created simplified radio-controlled scale models of these objects and demonstrated that not only could their models fly but generated an efficient amount of lift to be seen as an aircraft more advanced than the first planes invented back during the early 1900's.

Number 3: The 18th Century Robots

Referred to as the Jaquet Droz Automata, three robots with incredible realism were created by the Jaquet Droz family to showcase the incredible ability that mechanisms and clockwork can have in the design of automata. Many experts regard these robots as the ancient ancestors of the modern day computer and, given the tools and specifics used in the creation, showcase that early man has had the ability to create automata since the first mechanical clocks were invented in 723 A. D.

The three robots are known as the Musician, The Draughtsman and The Writer and each contains incredible abilities and performances.

The Musician is a robotic creation modelled after a female organ player. Interestingly enough, the robot performs live music that has not been recorded or played through a music box, but rather, the robot plays a genuine, custom-built instrument by pressing the keys with her fingers. Detailed movements of her chest show her breathing as her head and eyes follow the movement of her fingers.

The Draughtsman is a robotic creation modelled after a young child and is capable of drawing four different images with incredible detail; these images include a portrait of Louis the 15th, a royal couple, a dog with the caption "My doggy" and an elaborate scene of Cupid driving a chariot being pulled by a butterfly. Other details of the robot include using a special system that code the movements of the hand in two dimensions to reprogram the robot for new images as well as the ability to lift the pencil. The robot, Draughtsman, will also move in his chair and occasionally, at near random intervals, blow on the pencil to remove dust.

The last robotic creation is known as The Writer and is regarded as being the most complex of the three automata. The Writer is capable of easily being programmed to write any custom text up to 40 letters long. The text can be coded by selecting letters on a wheel one by one as the robot comes to life using a goose feather to write, of which he will ink on his own from time to time, including a shaking of the wrist to prevent ink from spilling across the page.

Considering the fact that these robotic creations can effectively function without the need of electricity and, rather, with the use of tools available to early civilizations, it has often been used as a source of argument for the availability of advanced technologies for early human cities and developments.

Number 4: The Saqqara Bird

It was very common in the old days of Egypt for children to possess intricately carved wooden toys not much different to toys found today. Interestingly enough, the discovery of the Saqqara artifact puts many ideas into question on whether or not the object was a toy or that of evidence of ancient aircraft during 200 BCE. In an 1898 excavation at the Pa Di Imen tomb located in the town of Saqqara, Egypt, there were discovered strange bird shaped artifacts made out of sycamore wood and incredibly well-preserved. These artifacts depict a bird at the front; however, the rest of the body seems similar in design to that of a modern day charter plane rather than a bird.

Located atop the bird appears to be one single large wing, commonly seen in modern taildragger planes, whereas the back of the artifact shows what appears to be a similar design to a rudder that flattens out at the back in a vertical position. Further evidence of the Ancient Egyptian gods wielding advanced technologies is the fact that the bird face used for the Saqqara bird is that of a falcon, an image commonly used to depict many of the Egyptian gods and their power. Further evidence was established when aerodynamics expert, Simon Sanderson, tested an exact replica model of the carved bird in a modern wind tunnel. Even without a tailplane, rudder or flaps, the model generated four times the gliders own weight in lift, proving indefinitely that even without the use of modern day equipment, scaled up, the carved image could glide on its own.

When Simon Sanderson added a stabilizing tailplane to the carved wooden figure and tested it in a flight simulator, it was able to fly quite well and controlled with an ease that rivals in comparison to many aircraft built today. In his paper, Simon wrote that "modern technology has proved beyond all doubt that it could have flown." Despite this substantial evidence and research, many experts claim Simon Sanderson as forging results or even go as far as claiming that perhaps the wooden bird is nothing more than an elaborate hoax placed there during its discovery.

Number 5: The Dropa Stones

Discovered in 1962, by a man named Chu Wenming, the Dropa Stones were described as being a series of 716 circular stone discs that were dated as far back as 12,000 years ago, predating the first human civilizations. The stones were inscribed with tiny Hieroglyphic-like images that detailed a strange story of possible extraterrestrial origin. This story was supposedly translated to state that a strange species of beings had descended from a cloud in the sky, after realizing they were unable to ascend back up to the skies, they were then forced to begin to adapt and live on the planet. The story then detailed that, unaware of the nature these strange beings and their intentions, the local Han Chinese began to hunt them down and kill them.

According to the researcher Chu Wenming, the images seemed similar to that of modern day UFO sightings and flying saucers. Believing these stones to be evidence of the record of ancient extraterrestrial contact, in 1962, Chu Wenming published his findings to the archaeological community only for it to be ridiculed and discredited and later cause Chu Wenming to go to Japan in a self-induced exile of shame. Further information surrounding the stones were described in the Soviet magazine, known as Sputnik, that claimed a handful of these stones were sent from a museum to Moscow. Supposedly a doctor, by the name of Vyatcheslav Saizev, describes an experiment in which the discs were placed on special turntables where they began to vibrate or hum in an unusual repeating rhythm as if they possessed an electric current passing through them. Since these experiments and findings, the stones have gone missing only for them to have never surfaced again.

This could very well mean that not only were the stones legitimate in their details and evidence of ancient extraterrestrial contact, but that efforts were made by the Chinese and Russian government to cover up these strange artifacts and prevent them from ever being seen again. Many people in the ancient alien community speculate that perhaps these discs could have contained a massive amount of digital data and could be the smoking gun evidence of ancient extraterrestrial contact.

Reasons Advanced Civilisations Existed

Though there are many people in the alien community that believe that not only were our ancestors significantly more advanced than us, but that perhaps advanced civilizations flourished in the past and were far more abundant and capable than of the current modern age. Originally seen as nothing more than a ridiculous conspiracy theory, the idea of an advanced prehistoric age has come to the forefront in archeological discoveries and even more frequently in the alien community. What many people often struggle to understand; however, is what could have been the particular cause for these advanced civilizations to have existed in the past and why it is that these ancient technologies have been lost to us in the modern day. In this section, we will be going over five reasons as to why advanced civilizations may have existed and the reasons for why they no longer exist today.

Number 1: Alien Civilization Laborers

When discussing theories around the Annunaki, and other ancient alien references, there seems to be a resurfacing theme of labor when it comes to contact with our ancient ancestors and their supposed gods. In fact, cultures from all around the world detail how our ancestors would bring the gods gifts of precious minerals such as gold, silvers and various metals. This has led many conspiracy theorists amongst the ancient alien community to believe that perhaps the gods of the ancient times were merely extraterrestrial life forms looking to convince the population of the Earth to work for them and gather precious minerals to be used and harvested for their own technologies. This theory would make sense from a logistics standpoint.

Given the fact that aliens most likely would have originated from an environment vastly different from that of our planet, it could be a very real possibility that entering the Earth's atmosphere and walking amongst its environment could be incredibly hazardous to any extraterrestrial life. This could be due to either the variation in gravity on our planet to their home planet, the stressful atmospheric conditions of our planet or even viruses of which would be so foreign to the alien species that their immune systems would be completely unable to defend against our native diseases. This could very well mean that humans could have been used as a commanded labor force to retrieve these precious minerals and provide them to the ancient visitors.

Given the vast amount of evidence in regards to ancient cultures depicting the gods originating from the stars and sharing advanced knowledge, ancient civilizations could have had assistance from these extraterrestrial visitors and have been far more advanced than ever previously known, due to the alien visitors making an attempt to grow a competent labor force for their own personal objectives. If we analyze this theory, it would then begin to shed light on the fact that the first human cities that formed were caused by an organized religion and a requirement of workforce as seen in the Ancient Egyptian culture and Ancient Sumerian cities.

Number 2: Alien Soldiers For Conquer

Following this idea of possible laborers created by ancient alien civilizations, the concept of training soldiers for conquer is also a theory not completely out of the question. It could very well be that these ancient extraterrestrial visitors made contact with individual tribes of humans in the hopes of using them as vessels to conquer other human tribes. Evidence for this can be seen in the historical figure, Genghis Khan, of whom credited his intelligence and advancement in technologies to an incident he experienced as a child entering into a cave and encountering strange beings with elongated heads.

In fact, it was due to their insights that the great Genghis Khan not only conquered many parts of the known world, but to continue his reign over his country and establish civility, laws, social contracts and trade. A similar story can be seen in that of the legends of Atlantis. The Atlanteans were given gifts from the gods in technology and developments in the hopes of conquering the world and providing this domain for the gods; however, instead of conquering the surrounding nations, the Atlanteans instead became isolationist and began studying and developing further instruments of war in the hopes of defeating the gods themselves. This could be evidence that not only were the Atlanteans aware of their supposed god's true nature as a conquering extraterrestrial species, but that they turned against these visitors and suffered their wrath in return.

Number 3: Time Travelers From The Future

Many UFO researchers and members of the alien community have noticed an eerie similarity between the humanoid figures of the Grey Aliens and humans of the modern day. In fact, there seems to be so much of a similarity that evolutionarily it almost seems as if we share a common ancestor. This theory is a prominent theory in the time travel community of whom not only believe that perhaps we do share a common ancestor with the Grey Aliens but also that perhaps humans of the modern day might actually be the common ancestor of the Grey Aliens. This might be a confusing concept to grasp initially; however, the evidence is overwhelming. After Albert Einstein discovered the theory of special and general relativity, it became known that if an entity could travel faster than the speed of light, they would be able to not only travel through great distances in space, but also great distances in time.

Unfortunately, performing this action is no easy task. It was discovered, that the only way to travel faster than the speed of light, would be to use a theoretical bending in space-time known as gravitational waves. Luckily for us, this theory of gravitational waves was proven true rather recently. Back in 2014, the first measurements of gravitational waves were measured by analyzing the changes caused by two orbiting black holes. This means that not only is time travel possible within our universe, but that it most likely is a natural occurrence. This could very well mean that these supposed extraterrestrials are nothing more than our future counterparts traveling into the past to observe their early ancestors. It could very well be that first contact scattered all throughout human history is merely the cataloging of humanity itself.

This could be evidence of advanced civilizations having formed via information shared by our future counterparts in the hopes of either making attempts at increasing our rate of evolution or merely due to ensuring the stability of the timeline. This could also be a main explanation as to why these advanced civilizations no longer exist and any memory of them has been completely eradicated, most likely due to our future counterparts ensuring that the timeline does not change and that their impacts on the natural evolution of our species does not carry any drastic effects on our species.

Number 4: Humanity Restarting Over Again

There is a famous quote made by Albert Einstein, one of the greatest scientific minds of the modern age and a key figure in the era of the golden age of enlightenment in quantum physics. He states the following: "*I do not know with what weapons World War III will be fought, but World War IV will be fought with sticks and stones.*" This insight has led many conspiracy theorist communities to ask the question on whether or not this has been the first time we have discovered this deadly technology.

Could it be that humans are engaged in a cycle of self destruction and that, when our technology reaches a certain point, we act self destructively of which forces us to restart humanity all over again. Given the fact that fossils of the modern human have been found stretching as far back as 200,000 years into the prehistoric age and the first ancient civilizations did not form until roughly 10,000 years ago, this would then assume that there was a 190,000 year period in which humans did absolutely nothing. Of course, this could not be the case. It has become a very real possibility that perhaps nuclear arms and technology has been in an unbreakable loop for millenia and that perhaps we are merely nearing our end. It could very well be that these advanced ancient civilizations could be nothing more than a warning to our modern age that if we do not learn from our mistakes, we are doomed to repeat them.

Number 5: Non-Human Civilization

Though all of the previous theories spoken about have

only focused on the possibility of advanced human civilizations, this might not have been the case. It could very well be that the first advanced civilizations on the planet were not that of humans getting insight from extraterrestrials but rather from extraterrestrials themselves. There is an overwhelming amount of evidence in historical documents and artifacts of a certain race of Giants referred to as the Cyclopes. Now, of course, the existence of Giants are referenced in cultures from all around the world from the Norse, to the Greeks, to the Egyptians and so on, but the importance of the Cyclopes is unique in that there are still massive ancient cities that exist to this day that provide overwhelming evidence for these creatures having once flourished in the past.

Known in the archaeological community as Cyclopean Masonry, incredibly large megalithic structures exist that could not have been possible to create given the primitive technologies of the past. In fact, many historical Greek documents, from philosophers and historians from that time, recounted that the megalithic structures were created by the Cyclopes in an effort to demonstrate their incredible abilities and technological prowess. This could mean that perhaps the first extraterrestrial visitors that arrived on our planet used technology in genetic manipulation to allow them to live on the planet and not suffer from any hazardous environments or diseases, crafting for themselves gigantic forms and playing a key part in the evolution of human beings. Though many might regard this theory as absurd or impossible, more and more evidence is being uncovered every single day and it might not be long before the truth comes out.

Strange Alien Jungle Mysteries

It appears that the dense jungles of the world hide strange and wondrous mysteries that are not only difficult to explain but seem to defy preconceived notions about science, history and the world itself. In this section, we will be going over three mysterious jungle discoveries related to the existence and assistance of extraterrestrials that cannot be explained in an effort to help bring these peculiar discoveries to light and to better understand the impossible world around us.

Number 1: The Origin of The Prehistoric Stone Spheres Of Costa Rica

The Stone Balls were first referenced back in 1971 by famed ancient alien author, Erich Von Daniken, in his cult classic novel known as the "Chariots of the Gods". The original discovery of these stone spheres go as far back as the 1940's. Located and scattered throughout the jungles of Costa Rica, these spheres were originally found in the Delta of the Terraba River but followed as far away north as the Estrella Valley and as far south as the mouth of the Coto Colorado River. This appears to be no easy feat, however, as the objects were massive, most of them being as large as roughly two meters in diameter and weighing more than 16 metric tons. In Ancient Costa Rican myth, as well as evidence found by archaeologists, it was originally believed that these spheres served a strange purpose by matching constellations in the sky and that, according to these myths, represented the constellation of which the gods had arrived from.

The Ancient astronaut community believed that the spheres could have served as a primitive star map, depicting a very specific constellation as told by the ancient gods in an attempt to show us their home planet when the time was right. Unfortunately, the Costa Rican Stone Spheres, when discovered, were either moved from their original location by archaeologists and researchers or blown up by treasure seekers believing the stone spheres to contain ancient artifacts, priceless antiques or gold treasures that could be sold on the black market.

It is due to this that the true nature and archaeological

context of the scattered spheres is completely lost for the foreseeable future and, though there may be a handful of stones still in there original location, hundreds of others have been completely destroyed, removed or washed away by flooding in the region altogether. Even though the surviving stones could still prove to be useful regarding archaeological context and discovery, for some strange reason, the discovery has gone wildly unnoticed and completely ignored since its original finding back in the 1940's.

Number 2: Nazi Buildings Located In South America

There have always been odd conspiracy theories circling the internet relating to the possible creation of secret Nazi research bases in Antarctica, South America and even on the moon, that were constructed with the purpose of maintaining contact with extraterrestrial life and their technologies. Additionally, it was also believed, in rumor, that the Nazi leader, Adolf Hitler, had actually escaped death and instead fled Germany to these secret bases in the hopes of starting a new life and building up the Nazi regime once again. It did not take long for those rumors to become genuine worry after the United States launched an investigation into the claims of the death of the Nazi leader only for the Federal Bureau of Investigation to come to the unanimous and unified conclusion that Adolf Hitler's body was not recovered and the body originally believed to be the Nazi Leader's was nothing more than that of an SS officer.

Conspiracy theorists quickly began to make the majority of the leg work locating Adolf Hitler, and many other Nazi leaders, of whom had fled Germany shortly before the imminent demise of the Nazi party. Though many people believed these efforts to be made in vain, it did not take long for true evidence to surface after privately funded investigations were made into the Argentinian jungles. Archaeologists and conspiracy theorists worked together and discovered Nazi plans of systemized escape in efforts to funnel thousands of war criminals through Spain to areas in Argentina and Brazil. Though many historical facts are clouded in mystery, according to many of the conspiracy theorist findings, stories say that the Nazi officers, including Adolf Hitler, arrived by rubber dinghies off the southern coast of Patagonia.

Following this record, back in 2015, Argentinian archaeologists, led by researcher Daniel Schavelzon of the University of Buenos Aires, discovered three large buildings built by the Nazi regime deep within the Argentinian jungles. Located at the site were several German coins with dates between 1938 and 1944 as well as porcelain dishware engraved with writings that translated from German that stated "Made in Germany" as well as many Nazi symbols, including the Swastika, engraved into the sides of the buildings.

Not only were the buildings typical of German architecture, but they were discovered in a completely remote site that would have normally been inaccessible to the local population that could very easily cover up clandestine operations. Unfortunately, not much more could be discovered as it appeared obvious that the site had long since been abandoned and any hidden Nazi operations were most likely moved to another location. Given the fact that the Nazi regime had special projects that referenced the creation of many hidden locations from all around the world, it could be a very real possibility that the Nazi regime is still active to this day, slowly building its numbers and working in anonymity.

Number 3: The Amazon Rainforest Aliens

Surprisingly, reports of alien sightings and strange orbs of light have often been claimed in certain areas of the Amazon Rainforest that have been referred to as alien hotspots by certain extraterrestrial investigation communities and U.F.O. researchers. One of these hotspots, located near the Mamaus region of the Amazon, was known for having the highest frequency of strange sightings and extraterrestrial encounters. This proved to be the case when two British tourists were visiting the region and caught high definition footage of an alien presence.

According to Michael Cohen, a prominent paranormal and extraterrestrial investigator of whom first received the footage, the two tourists were spending time with a local family while preparing their camera to take high quality pictures of the local family to add to their photo album. As they turned the camera on, there was a sudden flash of light as they noticed a strange figure standing in the background. After reviewing the footage, a still image was taken that showed overwhelming proof of a Grey alien arching its back and standing in the forest behind them as an orb of light followed closely behind.

Many skeptics were quick to dismiss the footage as a hoax after they deemed the quality to be so defined and high detail that the image had to have been completely faked to get such a good quality picture, of which seems to be a rather ridiculous explanation for such overwhelmingly high quality evidence of the alien presence. Oddly enough, a few weeks after the event, the Brazilian government declassified a wide variety of secret high level files regarding extraterrestrial investigation made by the government and a team of secret investigators.

These files detailed an military operation known as Operation Prato that detailed evidence of the Brazilian government sending out military units to monitor and confirm an alien presence in the Mamaus region of the Amazon Rainforest, at the exact spot that the footage was taken by the British tourists only a few weeks prior to the declassification of the files. Though the Brazilian government had often denied the existence of Operation Prato in the past, it appears that after the footage went public, the government was unable to maintain the secret and declassified files regarding the matter; helping to solidify the evidence as official and not that of a hoax or edited picture.

Ancient Egyptians Encountered Aliens

Many people in the Ancient Alien conspiracy community have the firm belief that it could very well be a possibility that the ancient gods written about in legends could have actually been advanced alien life forms from other planets assisting with the technological and evolutionary advancements of human beings. One of the biggest pieces of evidence of these claims comes from the cradle of human civilization, Ancient Egypt, that made breakthroughs in the development of agriculture, science, medicine, mathematics and the construction of large cities and societies. In this section, we will be asking the question and delving into the vast array of evidence of the meddling of alien life forms in the early history on humanity. Did the Ancient Egyptians encounter an alien race?

The first piece of evidence to take a close look at is probably the most notable and obvious piece of evidence in the Ancient Alien community. The Great Pyramids of Giza are often reported as one of the greatest wonders of the world, and with this title, hold an air of mystery and curiosity. How were these megalithic structures constructed, for what purpose and to what end? Interestingly enough, even to this day, we really have no idea. Archaeologists and Egyptologists from all around the world have devoted their lives to the study of these structures but still can not seem to crack exactly how they were built. To this day, we have not been able to recreate these structures even on a much smaller scale with the same precision as our predecessors. Understanding this, how can such a technology to perform this incredible feat of engineering in a short 20 years have existed back then? In fact, the sheer size and number of blocks used, along with the workforce, is more than enough evidence of advanced technologies.

The Great Pyramid consists of roughly 2.3 million stone blocks, each weighing more than a car, ranging from 2.5 to 15 tons a piece. According to supposed receipts discovered in nearby tombs and areas regarding the pyramids, the Pharaoh recorded that only 20,000 workers built the Pyramid over the course of 20 years. Mathematically, this does not make much sense. If that turns out to be the case, according to these Ancient Egyptian records, then that would mean that a block was cut from the quarry, moved to the Pyramid, pushed up a ramp and then placed in its correct alignment within the span of two minutes and 30 seconds. This is a technological impossibility. Of course, given other questionable historical records such as that of the Hatshepsut problem, the Ancient Egyptian civilization have created forged documents and receipts in the past to cover up problems with ownership, timeline and creation. It could very well be possible that this forgery took place for the creation of the pyramids as well; given the timeline, workload and many other staggering pieces of evidence when it comes to theories and techniques of the formation of the pyramid and the fact that they just do not seem to add up.

Another piece of evidence of this potential forgery of documents along with advanced technologies is that of the creation of the Sphinx. What many people are not aware of is that the face of the Sphinx is so symmetrical that it is impossible to replicate completely in the modern day without using laser technology. This means that the left side of the face so accurately matches the other side that it is almost as if a perfect mirroring of the object was used, something impossible to replicate by hand, even with the most skilled craftsmen. There is only two different ways that such a feat could be accomplished in the modern age, by using an advanced laser system to help 3D print the object by carving out a perfectly symmetrical piece from a slab or to use a mold with molten rock to create the structure, a theory of which is what many Archaeologists have posited forward.

The problem with the molten rock theory, however, is the fact that new evidence shows that the Sphinx was most likely originally in the shape of a large Anubis, similar to statues found in recovered tombs to signal the Gateway to the Underworld and the Guardians. This means that the human-like face was carved down with perfect symmetry, something that is physically impossible to do without advanced technologies. Not only this, but there are a tremendous amount of documents from one of the previous Pharaohs claiming to have built the Sphinx with his own face on them since the beginning, proving that his account and claim are nothing more than forged documents to take credit for technologies that must have predated their civilization and had existed much longer than previously expected. Interestingly enough, despite the overwhelming evidence of these forged documents and the recreation of the Sphinx, many Archaeologists and Egyptologists refuse to accept these obvious pieces of the puzzle that help us to better understand possible human history.

One of the most overwhelming pieces of evidence can also be found by looking at these massive structures and the math used to construct them; the Royal Cubit. The Ancient Egyptian Royal Cubit is the oldest attested standard of measurement, dating further back then 4,000 B.C.E., making it one of man's earliest tools used in construction. The strange thing about this is not the age of the measuring system, but rather, the math behind it. The Egyptian Royal Cubit is exactly equal to Pi minus Phi squared. It uses a perfect measurement of well known mathematical discoveries in the modern age to get its perfect unit of measurement. Interestingly enough, this unit is a perfect subdivision of the circumference of the Earth. Many scholars will wrongly assume that the Egyptian Royal Cubit was measured by using the distance from the Pharaoh's elbow to his finger tip but that is far from the truth.

In fact, to get the Royal Cubit, The ancients measured the rate of precession, which is the rate of the slow wobble of the Earth's axis of which appears as the miniscule but obvious movement of the constellations along the horizon. If the Ancient Egyptians continued this measurement system for 72 years per single degree out of 360 degrees, of which would represent the perfect spherical shape of the Earth, then the ancients could easily measure the radius of the Earth by measuring one side of a six-sided polygon, of which was often used in their base 6 numbering system similar to old Sumerian counting systems.

This ultimately means that the Ancient Egyptians triangulated stars' positions with where they would appear in the future, relative to the horizon, according to the rate of precession, and so, related time to distance, which is required to measure a planet's latitude and longitude. This means that not only did the Egyptians base their measurement off of the subdivision of the Earth itself, but also mapped out the Earth's size, rotation, movements and even the latitude and longitude of the planet all the way back in 4,000 B.C.E.

or those that believe this could be impossible, the Pyramid at Giza uses this Royal Cubit measurement system and comes out to a perfect subdivision of Earth, being exactly 1 out of 172,800 units of the Earth's circumference. Not only this but oddly enough, the latitude and longitude of the Pyramid comes out to be exactly the Speed of Light. Something impossible to have known for such an ancient civilization without the help of advanced technologies.

So, if it is more than obvious that the Egyptians possessed help from an advanced alien race, who were these extraterrestrials and what evidence do we have with them meddling in the history of our species and entire planet.

The Egyptian Gods.

It seems obvious when you really look at Egyptian history that the supposed Egyptian Gods were nothing more than extraterrestrials assisting early human history. Early Egyptians lived in small villages and were not much more advanced compared to their simpler neighbors and nomads in the region. It was not until the first signs of idols made to the Egyptian Gods, or rather, evidence of the Egyptian Gods appearing, that the Egyptian civilization began to grow in refinement, complexity, agriculture, mathematics, science and labor. In Egyptian mythology, Osiris, Isis, Seth, and Nephthys came from the sky and had many children of whom became gods as well. Many of the Egyptian beliefs also focus on the stars and the belief that different stars in the night sky held significant importance to the old Egyptian Gods, being either a temple in the sky or the distance traveled to reach paradise in the afterlife.

One of the most compelling pieces of evidence made for the Egyptian Gods being advanced life forms was their obvious talents in genetic manipulation. It was known that the Egyptian Gods could change their form and take the forms of different animals, including human beings, but that their true forms were never known.

After the rampage of Bastet, to prove the power of the gods, the Egyptian gods gave a gift to humans to apologize for what had happened. This gift was the domesticated house cat, supposedly crafted by the gods to be the perfect companion to human beings. Something strange to note is that fossils of the domesticated cat do not exist predating Egypt. In fact, nothing connecting it to other cats exists in the planet and the only record of the oldest fossils only exist in Egypt after the major developments were made in agriculture and the establishment of the Egyptian religions.

Not only this, but cat behavior analysts have found that, unlike every other species in the world, cats have been the only species to co-evolve alongside humans rather than becoming domesticated fully. This most likely appeared due to the fact that cats began living alongside humans as agriculture developed and humans and felines grew a symbiotic relationship relative to said agricultural developments. This means that humans benefited from having cats living amongst our fields because they killed vermin and cats benefited from living with us because they got to eat a lot of vermin that was produced by our organized crops, almost as if our relationship is entirely unique to every other animal, similar to this concept of them being a gift provided by the Egyptian gods. Could it very well be that the domesticated cat is the perfect companion provided by advanced life forms eons ago?

The Bigfoot U.F.O Connection

There has always been speculation amongst the fringe topic community surrounding the coincidence between the strange sightings of a large ape-like creature, known commonly as Bigfoot or Sasquatch, and the sightings of Unidentified Flying Objects located in the same region. Though there are many that seem to refuse to engage in the conversation relative to this odd connection, there are important statistics to note about this strange correlation. In this section, we will be looking over data and analyzing the information as to the viability of the connection of Bigfoot and Unidentified Flying Objects.

After the creation of the independent organization known as the Mutual Unidentified Flying Object Network, or M.U.F.O.N. for short, a lot of information was gathered about various sightings of UFOs and extraterrestrial activity over several years about different facts and connections made. Among these connections, the M.U.F.O.N. organization made a startling realization, there was mainly only three different extraterrestrial types that existed.

The first most commonly sighted extraterrestrial was referred to as the "Greys", a species that was on average to be 3 to 4 feet tall, grey-skinned with large black eyes, small mouths, and large oval-shaped heads. They would commonly appear to be very humanoid in nature and are the most recognizable figures of alien life across popular media and mainstream science fiction works.

The second most commonly seen extraterrestrial sighting were referred to as the Nords. The Nordic aliens were named as such given the fact that they appeared to be eerily similar to the description of old Norse gods and of the Scandinavian people at large. Most witness accounts described these strange Nordic aliens as having a milky white complexion, brilliant blue eyes, white hair and dressed in the apparel of white clothing but appear, in all other regard, to look completely human. It is important to keep these two extraterrestrial sightings in mind because we will later be coming back to them, but most important we need to look at the third most common E.T. sighting.

The Sasquatch.

Oddly enough, it appeared that the third most common sighting of an alien being was that of a Bigfoot. Many people of whom encountered strange UFO sightings wrote witness reports of saucers landing and a Bigfoot coming out, or encountering a Bigfoot in the forest only for it to disappear like a ghost and for, moments later, to see a nearby unidentified flying object begin to immediately take off into the sky. These cases also do not include single encounters with the Sasquatch and only include reports regarding a definitive extraterrestrial account.

Could it be then that the Sasquatch creature is another race of extraterrestrials visiting our planet? Are they most fascinated with forests than other areas given the fact that the majority of Sasquatch sightings are around forested locations? Looking at other strange parallels in connection with ancient mythologies appears to surface a strange and startling discovery.

Many past ancient alien enthusiasts have made the potential connection between aliens and Gods, positing forth the theory that perhaps the gods of the past were merely aliens guiding and influencing the evolution of our species. But another connection that has yet to be made has been found by looking at the ancient mythologies of past human civilizations. The Sasquatch eerily fits the description of the Giants.

Scattered throughout mythologies around the world is reference to creatures similar to that of the gods but often regarded differently due to their large size. The Greeks referred to them as Titans, the Jews as the Nephilim, the Norse as Giants, even myths of the isolated Easter Island inhabitants and their religions talked about Giants first inhabiting the region and constructing the massive megalithic structures referred to as Easter Island Heads. In fact, many megalithic structures from around the world are surrounded by myths of Giants constructing them, including ancient Hieroglyphics depicting Giants walking amongst Ancient Egyptians and their constructions. Many different religions, cultures and mythologies from around the world provide information of their definitions and descriptions of these Giants of that past that fit the modern day descriptions of the Sasquatch today.

So, what do these ancient myths tell us about the Giants?

The only record that provides the most detailed account of stories of Giants inhabiting the forests alongside accounts of their special abilities comes from the legends and myths surrounding a mystical and enigmatic figure known as Merlin. Merlin wrote in countless details about a race of Giants that appeared to be ape-like but were far more evolutionarily advanced compared to the human race and had been around since the time before the humans. They predominantly lived in forest areas and had the ability to travel between different realms between the Earth and other various worlds. Their descriptions, provided by Merlin, also appear to match that of the modern day Sasquatch including descriptions in size, hair color, behavior and their fascination with the forests of our world.

Most important of all, however, is the fact that these creatures that Merlin encountered had the ability to travel interdimensionally between worlds using pockets and hidden areas on the Earth that allowed them to travel between great distances, similar to that of a secret wormhole or passageway in design.

Interestingly enough, the idea of Giants traveling between realms is not all that new and has a strange similarity to the old Norse mythologies. Referred to as the Jotunns, the Giants lived in two separate realms that connected at the Earth and fought against the old Norse gods in terrible battles. This idea of Gods versus Giants is also not new in regards to Norse mythology. This is also seen in the Gods fighting against Titans in Greece, or the flood of the ark in the bible that was caused by God to destroy the Nephilim.

But with Norse mythology there is an added level of strange detail. The Norse told of three different races. The first that we all know of is the humans. We live in the realm referred to as Midgard. In the realm known as Jotunheim lives the Giants, described to be large and hairy to be able to survive in the cold frosts of their world. In the realm of Asgard are the Norse gods and in the realm of Svartalfheim is the home of the Dwarves. Here, we make a startling comparison.

The three most common sighted extraterrestrials fit the definitions of the old Norse mythology of beings from other realms. The Dwarves in Norse mythology were also known as Dark Elves. Why is this? Because they had grey skin. In many depictions of the Dwarves, they also appeared to have large black eyes, small mouths, large oval shaped heads and were roughly 3 to 4 feet tall. They match the exact descriptions of modern day Grey aliens. Not only this but the Dwarves were known to be masters of technology and helped to craft the hammer of Thor, a Norse god, by utilizing the material in high density located at the center of a dying star, proving they had intergalactic means of travel. Could it be that the Dwarves in Norse mythology were the Grey aliens?

The second most common alien sighting, known as the Nords, exactly matches that of the Norse gods; possessing milky white skin, blue eyes and an overall human-like appearance. And lastly, the Norse mythologies of the Giants directly matches that of the modern day Bigfoot sightings.

After understanding and making these strange connections, we find that the most important question begins to surface. What could this mean? Is it possible that perhaps our understanding of alien life has been wrong this entire time? That perhaps these beings are not extraterrestrial but interdimensional?

More evidence is provided given the fact that not only is there undoubtedly a link between these Sasquatch creatures and sightings of Unidentified Flying Objects, but the fact that so many reports of these two other alien species so closely match the Norse religion and their information regarding their mechanisms of travel, which was the ability to use a rainbow bridge that could take them between realities.

This rainbow bridge, or rather, a bridge using the prism of light, seems so familiar to early concepts of a wormhole theory known as the Einstein-Rosen bridge. The ability to warp space time enough to manipulate gravitational waves and create an interdimensional means of travel which would, in turn, allow the manipulation of light waves simultaneously. Though we may not have all the answers, there seems to be an obvious missing key to the information provided. If the Sasquatch correlation proves that there are other interdimensional species visiting the Earth and using it as a meeting place, or rather, as a neutral ground, then could there still be a battle raging between these advanced life forms to this day? Are there other potential species visiting as well? If this is truly an interdimensional means, then given the ideas of Multiverse theory, could there be a potential infinite number of variations of ourselves amongst these universes and that is what we are witnessing?

Perhaps these Grey aliens, these Sasquatch creatures and these Nord-like advanced races are merely different potential evolutionary pathways we could have taken, of which would account for the reasons as to why each and every one of these alien races appear to be so humanoid in nature. Perhaps they were once human, and perhaps we share some common ancestor in our variant histories.

The United Kingdom's Area 51

The United States military base, known as Area 51, is known all across the world as being a hotspot of alien conspiracy as well as a possible research base housing extraterrestrial spacecraft while attempting to work at reverse engineering further alien technologies that have been recovered by the United States military. What many alien enthusiasts are not aware of, however, is that the United Kingdom has its own version of Area 51. The Rudloe Manor has been shrouded in mystery sinces its first uses with the United Kingdom military operations, mysteries that have only deepened as new evidence and theory comes to light. In this section, we will be exploring the vast complex conspiracy surrounding Rudloe Manor, also known as the United Kingdom's Area 51.

The history of Rudloe Manor started from very humble beginnings. Originally created as a bath stone mining station, the area that would later become Rudloe Manor was worked and designed to mine bath stone from the region to be used in massive building projects utilizing the material and its ability to be cut in any direction, a property that other layering stones do not have. This led to larger scale projects and cheaper means of production, of which worked to help build hospitals, different forms of housing and other major construction projects across the United Kingdom.

It was not until the start of World War II that Rudloe Manor gained its use in military operations, as the tunnels from the existing bath stone mine were at a prime location to store ammunitions and other material after the relentless strategies by the Nazi regime that led to massive bombings of above ground facilities. These tunnels, as well as other large caverns that burrow deep into the ground, helped to create a safe and stable natural bunker as it was merely used as a central ammunition depot at the start of the war but soon, the area found itself to be a major control center used by the Royal Air Force.

This led to the creation of further operations within the underground facilities of the Rudloe Manor in 1940 that included The Operations Room, The Filter Room and then finally the Shadow Factory. It is this collection of rooms that would later lead to the formation of an alien research base after the end of

World War II.

The Operations Room was essentially used as a military command center, establishing covert protocols on the handling of sensitive information and issuing out military commands to the Royal Air Force and establishing secret clandestine projects. The Filter Room acted as an intelligence filter, hence where it got its name, that served to establish a complex sorting system that helped to provide intelligence regarding enemy operations and further sensitive information and documents with such a secure filtering system that no leaks of information would have ever been possible from this Filter Room.

These two rooms, however, dwarf in comparison to the importance of the Shadow Factory. The Factory was originally established under the belief that a secret underground facility with the ability to create aircraft was necessary in the event that the Nazi forces continued their bombing assaults and destroyed factory productions of aircraft. This led to the creation of a complete underground facility with the incredible ability to produce entire aircraft in an assembly line from nothing but raw materials deep underground. Though the factory was claimed to have never been in operation, this would soon change during the 1950's.

After, what alien enthusiasts refer to as a definitive UFO incident, Rudloe Manor was then seen as a hotspot for alien activity and a control center for further investigations. This incident occurred as Royal Air Force Pilots returned from a bombing raid and encountered unidentified flying objects. Though the details around this incident are unknown, released reports provide further information claiming that Winston Churchill himself asked for the event to be covered up to prevent mass panic. This would develop into its own team of investigators from the Joint Intelligence Committee at the Rudloe Manor, within the Operations Room, as weekly reports would then be filed regarding the presence of extraterrestrials and the military's involvement.

Further leaked information began spreading that the underground Shadow Factory soon became used as a potential reverse engineering facility as the Royal Air Force had supposedly recovered a crashed alien spaceship that was being studied and held in the underground facility.

Interestingly enough, these rumors are further confirmed by, the James Bond equivalent of the alien world, Nick Pope, of whom had used to work for the British Ministry of Defence and was tasked by the government to study and gather further information and research relative to unidentified flying objects, the alien presence and their potential threat to national security. Pope would later go on to be an advocate for the disclosure projects with the hopes of the UK government releasing further documents relative to their findings of extraterrestrial activity but would later go on to say that mysteriously all of the files pertaining to the 1950's operations at Rudloe Manor that concerned alien activity was destroyed and unable to be recovered. Despite this unfortunate turn of events, further documents had later been released to the British National Archive that provided proof and evidence of the alien investigations and clandestine operations held at Rudloe Manor at this time, provided by the help of Nick Pope and his efforts at alien disclosure.

These clandestine operations included a wide array of alien reports that spanned over 5,000 documents, as well as famous events that had been covered up by the British government. The list of these events include a near collision report of a 737 airplane almost colliding with an unidentified flying object with statements from the captain and first officer, an alien response team investigating and recovering a crashed UFO at the Berwyn Mountains in Wales, full detailed investigative reports of the Western Isles incident that many locals claimed to have heard a loud explosion over the Atlantic confirming the incident to be of extraterrestrial origin, the 14 minutes of supposedly missing footage from the Blue Streak Missile test launch that shows evidence of a craft landing and the presence of a spaceman as described in the report, and many other incredible discoveries that seemed too frightening to be true.

Of course, these reports and their details would lead many conspiracy theorists and alien enthusiasts to begin referring to Rudloe Manor as the U.K.'s area 51 and as a potential command center for black budget operations that would soon go above the clearance level of even the highest officials in the military, British government and clandestine operations.

As much as people might argue that this would be a stretch, the logistics and developments that had already been established at Rudloe Manor were more than prepared to undertake such a project and to become a completely self-reliant facility and factory capable of its own research, production and testing. What many critics and skeptics of this idea do not realize is the extent of the size and ability of Rudloe Manor's vast complex tunnel systems. The underground tunnels and facilities make up more than 2.2 million square feet. To get a sense of this scale, one should look towards one of the biggest warehouse production facilities in the world, Amazon's fulfillment center. 2.2 million square feet is more than twice the size of Amazon's Fulfilment center, of which works to be a massive warehouse that produces and houses the endless goods available at Amazon worldwide. Now imagine this level of production completely underground, self sufficient and twice as massive with the budget of the British military, additional black budget spending and an endless amount of Royal Air Force engineers that are capable of doing the impossible. The potential is nearly limitless.

Now, if we take into account the past 70 years and the massive amount of reports that total over 5,000 documents and investigations, that would mean the facility had the ability to investigate a report roughly once every 5 days, on top of the additional clandestine operations that existed throughout this time and the usage of the Manor for sensitive intelligence and military operations. These reports are also only made up of the surviving documents and shared intelligence with the National Archive that are still around from that era. According to various sources and those within the intelligence community, many other reports, investigations and further informational documents had been destroyed to prevent any further leaked information of which could mean an additional tremendous amount of evidence for the search of alien activity and alien disclosure that are lost forever. The scale of this performance had to have already been massive and well underway.

It is also important to remember that information at the Rudloe Manor went through high levels of filtering processes, and so, forged documents would not have been created or stored at the facility. Many skeptics claim that the released documents supplied to the National Archive are merely bogus documents that work to spread misinformation amongst the general public; however, given the strict protocols that had already existed amongst the Joint Intelligence Committee and further witness accounts from Ex-British Ministry of Defence agent, Nick Pope, this seems to be the most improbable explanation for the release of these 1950's documents and archived information.

What is even more interesting about this case is that even though the Site 1 of the Rudloe Manor base has been decommissioned and no longer within military use. The Site 3 buildings along with the vast underground tunnel complex is still used and hidden by the British government and Royal Air Force. These tunnels were stated as being repurposed with the ability to house British politicians and other high clearanced personnel during the event of a nuclear strike and to be completely self-reliant and independent with vast established systems to live indefinitely underground. This could be further confirmation of the abilities of the Shadow Factory and its potential of vast production, self-reliance and pre-existing infrastructure spanning nearly 7 decades of developments.

UFO Encounters Covered Up

As we face a tremendous amount of new reports of sightings of unidentified flying objects every single year, with over two thousand sightings in 2018 alone, it is no wonder then that many of these incredible events can go without being noticed by the general public despite incredible levels of detail, evidence and proof of the experience and what it means for the future of our planet. In this section, we will be discussing 4 UFO encounters and experiences that you most likely have never even heard about until now.

Number 1: Hangzou UFO Sighting

With many sightings of unidentified flying objects, it becomes apparent that not only do skeptics try their hardest to disprove that what was seen was an actual alien presence but that nothing was even in the air in the first place. This appears to be an impossible task when discussing the Hangzou UFO sighting. Back in 2010 on the 7th of July, the Xiaoshan airport located in Hangzhou, China, ceased all operations and was temporarily shut down as a strange anomaly hovered over the airport. The first witnesses of the unidentified flying object was a flight crew preparing to land at the airport at approximately 8:40 PM. They quickly notified the air traffic control department as the object was not only a safety risk for all incoming flights preparing to descend but appeared to be strange in nature and could have possibly been an extraterrestrial craft.

Within minutes, the Chinese Aviation Authorities responded by grounding all outbound flights and diverting any inbound flights away from the airport in fear of the craft's abilities. After an hour, the craft disappeared and the flight traffic control quickly resumed functions. As an investigation continued into the incident, it turned out that roughly an hour prior to the event, others had spotted and taken pictures of a strange UFO that appeared to have been surrounded in golden light and exhibiting a comet-like tail in the sky. Other witnesses reported that the object changed and then began emitting red and white rays of light in all directions.

Despite so many eyewitnesses and the fact that the object itself hovered over the airport for roughly an hour, only one photograph remains depicting the object, pointing to a possible cover up of the situation made by the Chinese government of whom released very few details of the investigation.

Number 2: Norwegian Spiral Anomaly

Lasting for over 10 minutes, a large strange spiral anomaly formed in the night skies above northern Norway and Sweden and was seen across a vast distance in a massive spectacle. The strange object appeared to have originated from a blue streak of light that began radiating in the sky in a perfect spiral shape with a darkened center almost as if it was appearing to be a wormhole being opened up in the night sky. Almost immediately, calls from all across the area began flooding the Norwegian Meteorological Institute as residents wanted to know what was going on and what they were witnessing above them. To provide a quick explanation and calm the minds of the individuals panicking from what they were seeing, a popular Norwegian astronomer posited that the sighting was nothing more than a fireball meteor in the sky burning up; however, this was quickly disproven as the object continued lingering in the sky for a much longer time than a fireball meteor of any kind could have persisted for.

To quickly supply an answer for the event as the public began to grow uneasy once more, the Norwegian Meteorological Institute began speculating that the event could have been nothing more than a rare Northern Lights event despite the fact that no such event existed and no proof for such a claim was ever put forward. Many UFO enthusiasts were the first to make the connections between the recent high energy experiments that were occuring at the Large Hadron Collider nearby and believed that the event being witnessed could have been that of a wormhole opening up or as evidence of extraterrestrial involvement attempting to make their presence known. Though many photographs and recordings of the event took place along with a tremendous amount of witness reports, an official explanation has yet to be offered by the Norwegian or Swedish government and it did not take very long before the incident faded into obscurity.

Number 3: Height 611 UFO Incident

During the reign of the Soviet Union, there was a tremendous amount of sightings and UFO incidents that were cast aside and forgotten about due to the fact that the government of the Soviet Union worked tirelessly to hide evidence of extraterrestrials from its citizens in fear of its people discovering that there were higher powers that extended beyond the power and control of the Soviet Union. Because of this, many of these incidents are not well known even amongst dedicated members and researchers of the alien community. One of these such incidents was that of the Height 611 UFO incident that occurred back in 1986, on the 29th of January, in the small town of Dalnegorsk. According to the residents of the town, a strange reddish orb of a massive size was spotted at around 8:00 P.M. that had passed over the town.

This reddish orb was described as being as half as large as the moon overhead and to have appeared to have been similar in color and luminescence to that of a dark red flame. Eyewitnesses also noted that as the object flew parallel to the ground, it made no noise of any kind as it passed over, something that seemed impossible to accomplish with even the most advanced aircraft imaginable. Using specified witness time frames and the flight path of the object, investigators calculated that the orb flew at approximately 34 miles per hour and that it was flying roughly 700-800 meters above the ground.

As the object continued its flight path overhead, it suddenly began descending quickly and crashed into the side of the mountains located near the town. Oddly enough, every witness reported that not only did the object crash into the side of the mountain and appear to have exploded, or spread temporarily as a natural wildfire before dissipating and completely disappearing, but that as it crashed, it made no sound whatsoever, of which is a feat that is impossible to accomplish regardless of any advancements made in flight capabilities as it seems to defy the fundamental laws of physics themselves. Further investigation yielded interesting results as some rocks at the impact site had drops of lead that had previously been molten before solidifying on the rocks in the cold. Not only this but rare Earth metals were also recovered in the vicinity that were not naturally found in any types of deposits on the mountain previously. Unfortunately, the pictures taken by the investigators at the time, when later developed, turned out to be blank, almost as if they had been swapped out entirely and replaced with fresh film in an effort to cover up the evidence gathered at the location of impact. The official explanation provided by the Soviet Union, at the time, was that a meteorite had recently impacted the site and was the cause of the strange findings of the rare Earth metals and strange chemical composites; however, the provided explanation had failed to explain the eyewitness accounts of the event as well as the fact that sightings of strange red orbs landing on the mountainside would continue at the site over the next few years.

Number 4: The Close Encounters of Cussac

Though there are a tremendous amount of reported cases of eyewitness accounts of unidentified flying objects, it is very rare for eyewitnesses to report a direct sighting of an alien presence or extraterrestrial lifeform seen in clear detail during the event. This appears to not be the case when analyzing the close encounters of the Commune of Cussac, located in France. On the 19th of August, back in 1967, two children, a 13 year old boy and his 9 year old sister, ran to the police and alerted them to a strange sighting. They claimed that, as they were watching the cows in a nearby field, they noticed that there appeared to be four small people that were completely covered in a weird dark material and stood at roughly 47 inches tall. At first, they were not afraid of these strange people and originally thought it was other children around their age but began panicking when they noticed these strange beings suddenly begin to rise in the air and float up towards a metal disk-like object floating above them that was no more than roughly 15 feet in diameter.

At first, the officers didn't know what to make of the kids' story but noticed that the children appeared to be truly fearful as they continued to describe the scene in vast detail. Quickly, the officers followed the children to the sighting and noticed that there appeared to be a strange sulphur smell in the air near where the object was seen to have been hovering and that a large patch of dried grass had suddenly appeared in the area. After the police filed the report of the incident, the French government stepped in and conducted their own private investigations of the event and have yet to release any gathered information or investigation details. As time went on, the story died down and the government felt compelled to keep all gathered details of the investigation a secret and refused to acknowledge the cases existence up until March of 2007 when the French government released hundreds of declassified UFO investigations on their government website over 40 years after the event.

Paranormal

Cursed Objects
Around The World

Given the fact that no one knows the true nature of how a curse can occur, it has been a tale often fraught with mystery as much as terror. Though the ways an individual can be cursed can vary depending on culture, one thought that has always been the same is the ownership of an object and what that does to its owner. Often referenced throughout the history of a number of different cursed objects, of which have brought nothing but horror to its new home, there seems to be a retelling of these same themes to this day in modern tales of cursed objects that still find themselves in the ownership of families filled with misfortune. In this section, we will be going over six of these cursed objects that many might not take a second glance at and assume that they are nothing more than a normal everyday possession.

Number 1: The Mirror
At Myrtles Plantation

The location of a former plantation home found in St. Francisville, down in Louisiana, is often reported by the locals and paranormal researchers as one of the most haunted houses in the United States. Surrounding the land are numerous tales and local myths that report strange and violent histories that many people believe contributed to the properties terrible hauntings. One such myth is that of the Cursed Mirror at the Myrtles Plantation residency.

According to the legend, many years ago when the home was still an operating plantation with a variety of slave families, there were many slaves of whom practiced black magic and voodoo spells that were used to aid them in their goals. One night, as the owners of the plantation home were preparing for a meal, a slave of the plantation had created a special concoction to poison the family and had slipped the poison into the owner's food during their meal.

The entire family began complaining of terrible aches and pains and all died shortly thereafter. This was not enough for the angered slave; however, as the slave grabbed hold of one of their many mirrors used as a vanity and performed a special ritualistic ceremony to trap the souls of the family inside the large mirror. Oddly enough, one of the mirrors, believed to have been used by the family many years ago and found in the home tucked away in a back room, is often reported at the center of the hauntings for anyone of whom lives at the residency.

Many people have reported seeing hand prints against the mirror, as if someone had been resting their hand against it, only before shortly disappearing without any marks or fingerprints. Strange markings and symbols will often appear as well with no explanation before dissipating. One such owners have even gone as far as claiming that they had once seen figures dressed in old fashioned clothes standing in the reflection and screaming to be let out. The mirror still resides at the old Myrtles Plantation to this day.

Number 2: Annabelle, The Raggedy Ann Doll

Almost everyone used to own a Raggedy Ann doll back in its heyday, along with a Raggedy Andy doll to match your set. Some of these dolls can even go for as much as almost 1,000 U.S. dollars and it appears that several different companies sold several different variations of these incredibly popular designs. In the case of two paranormal researchers and self proclaimed demonology experts; however, the Raggedy Ann doll holds a very special place for them in a locked display case fitted and reinforced with a strong encasing metal.

This is due to the fact that their Raggedy Ann doll was recovered in a terrible haunting case of which they investigated many years ago. The doll was named Annabelle and displayed impossible characteristics that led its previous owners to suspect that it was cursed. It had the ability to move on its own, tap against objects, write terrifying messages and even supposedly speak out at random times. After the two paranormal researchers came, they took the doll away and locked it up in a display case to prevent it from ever being released again. This doll would later go on to inspire the Annabelle movie franchise and is often at the center of strange paranormal investigations.

Number 3: The Hands
Resist Him Painting

The artist, Bill Stoneham, was often known by those closest to him for creating life-like paintings that held a sense of photorealism based off of memories from his childhood or actual photographs taken by his parents many years ago. One day, as he put paint to canvas and painted a strange image that would later go on to be his most popular piece ever created, he would find that his own creation would come to life in the most terrifying way. The painting was later known as the Hands Resist Him Painting and portrayed an image of a photograph that had been taken back when Bill Stoneham was a child, standing alongside one of his childhoods friends as his parents snapped the picture. Interestingly enough, upon closer examination of the photograph, Bill Stoneham noticed that in the reflection against the window pane in the original photograph, there had been what looked like a pair of hands stretching out towards him.

He decided to add the image into his painting believing that perhaps it was nothing more than an awkward reflection from one of the parents standing behind the camera. It appears that after making this decision, Bill Stoneham inadvertently turned the painting into a haunted item. The painting has since been reported by owners and enthusiasts of the painting to be terribly haunted and to have been associated with several people of whom have already passed away. Back in 2000, the painting was put on E-Bay along with a detailed story of how it was haunted and the fates of the past owners. The painting is still on the market.

Number 4: The Haunted
Wedding Dress

Back in 1914, an old rumor was told that led many to believe a strange wedding dress was haunted by a woman in white that would visit those of whom owned the dress. The rumor claimed that back in 1849, there was a woman by the name of Anna Baker, of whom was born to a rich family in the state of Pennsylvania and had fallen madly in love with a low class iron worker. Unfortunately for Anna, her father refused to allow her to marry a man from a lower class and completely forbade the wedding from ever taking place. If Anna and the iron worker were to ever marry, then it would mean Anna would be forced to live a penniless life with nothing to show for it as her father would have completely cut her off.

The Iron worker refused to allow this to happen and it appeared that the wedding had been completely called off from ever happening, despite Anna having already bought the wedding dress for the event. The father had believed that after a few years Anna would completely forget about the whole ordeal and marry within her own class. This turned out to not be the case as Anna baker would eventually go on to live the remainder of her life completely single and never dating ever again, passing away in 1914. Since her passing, it appears that her wedding dress has been cursed with her presence as those that visit the house of which she lived in, that was later turned into a museum, will often report seeing strange apparitions walking about wearing the wedding dress along with the dress itself often moving on its own inside of its display case.

Number 5: The Anguished Man Painting

Although the story seems a little hazy on the specifics, a man by the name of Sean Robinson from Cumbria, England, reportedly is in the possession of the most haunted painting of all time. According to his own personal account, Sean Robinson had purchased a painting that depicted a man, made entirely out of blood, screaming in terrible pain and would often hang it up in his bedroom. He found that every night that he had had the painting hung up in his room, he would see terrifying images as well as hearing strange and unexplainable noises. When Sean Robinson looked more into who created the painting, he discovered that the previous artist had made the reds of the painting more realistic by actually incorporating his own blood and that, shortly after finishing this painting, he had taken his own life and passed away close to the canvas. After hearing this story, Sean Robinson believed the painting to be overwhelmingly haunted and has since kept it locked away at a hidden location.

Number 6: The Cursed Phone Number

Although it might sound like something out of a chilling horror movie, it appears that a Bulgarian phone number was at the center of rumors for being a haunted and cursed number. It appears that every person of whom was given the phone number, during its 10 year period of being in public use, had almost immediately passed away after receiving the number in a terrible and horrifying manner. Many of which were victims of random and violent crimes of whom the killer was never found. Though many might scoff at the idea of a cursed phone number, it appeared that the Bulgarian mobile phone company treated the reports with a serious precaution and, after the last gruesome murder of a victim of whom was provided that number, the company completely suspended that number from ever being used again. Even if you ask the mobile company to provide you with that phone number, paying for a special custom digit, they will refuse the number no matter the cost, which has only helped to keep the rumors of the cursed phone number alive and well.

Demonic Entities
From Around The World

In all religions and mythologies from around the world, there appear to be strange tales of evil spirits and malevolent entities referred to as demons. The names of these creatures may vary and their behaviors, at times, can be completely unpredictable. In this section, we will be going over 5 different demonic entities from around the world and what they are capable of doing.

Number 1: The Djinn

According to the ancient scriptures seen throughout the Middle East, the Djinn are often referred to as the People of the Fire and seem to be as old as the universe itself. Scholars have noted that the word Djinn itself most likely comes from the arabic root word "Jann", a word to which roughly translates to mean "to hide" or "to conceal," which gives us a clue as to the nature of the Djinn of which were often regarded as creatures of whom would attempt to conceal themselves from man. The Quran then clarifies that the existence of the Djinn first came about during the act of the creation of the universe and that the Djinn came into existence after being crafted from a smokeless fire, similar to that of electricity and much purer energy.

These stories, in fact, match that of the Judaism interpretation of the creation of Lucifer, of whom was also crafted from fire and not that of light similar to other angels. The Djinn were then described as being more accurately referred to as, the People of the Fire and that they would exist in a plane that rested slightly above ours but still within our world, slightly out of the reach of any of our natural senses. Additional information as to the origin and spreading of the Djinn get a little hazy thereafter, but references are made of the Djinn assisting ruthless kings and rulers and even helping with the building and construction of many cities and places of immense power. It is hard to refer to a Djinn as a demon as the Quran and other scriptures will often differentiate between the two as the scripture specifies that a good Djinn is referred to as a Djinn but a bad and malicious

Djinn is often just referred to as a demon. According to these scriptures, the Djinn are similar to man in that they possess the ability of free will and are even judged for their actions at the end of their lives.

Number 2: The Snallygaster

Although the creature might seem like a strange amalgamation of many different mythological creatures all put into one, the sightings behind that of the Snallygaster creature have been reported since the first German immigrants landed in the area of Central Maryland back in the 1730's. The first witness accounts of the creature came from these isolated German communities that claimed they were being attacked and stalked by a monster they referred to as the Schneller Geist, of which later became Snallygaster to the other immigrants in the region. Witnesses described the monster as having the features of a bird, the features of a siren, and the nightmarish designs of a demon and a ghoul mixed in one.

The creature was detailed as being half-reptile, half-bird, equipped with a metal beak lined with saw-like teeth, the tentacles of an octopus and had the ability to fly down from the sky and pick up and carry off with its victims. Other stories claimed that the monster was capable of attaching its suction cup tentacles to the face of an individual and slowly suck out all of the blood from their body. Reports of the creature seem to end by the end of the 1700's as many of those in the isolated communities claimed to have used stars with seven points on them to ward off the creature away. The complete disappearance of the creature did not prevent stories of the monster from surfacing all throughout the area through rumors and myth. Back in the early 1900's a local news outlet perpetuated a massive hoax report that detailed the monster attacking citizens all over the town of which eventually caused many different citizens to write letters to Theodore Roosevelt to help hunt down and take down the beast. Ever since this event, mention of the creature has faded away and the Snallygaster is only known as an old myth of a monster in the region.

Number 3: The Snarly Yow

In the past, there have been many strange claims reporting that of creatures known as "The Shadow People", seemingly made entirely out of nothing but a shadowy substance. Interestingly enough, it appears that in West Virginia, a similar creature appears to be the case for strange shadow-like canine creatures referred to as the Snarly Yow. The Snarly Yow is described as being similar to that in design to a large wolf with glowing red eyes, but made entirely out of nothing but shadows and capable of moving at incredible fast speeds. According to a witness report in the region of West Virginia, a hunter went out into the Appalachian Mountains on a camping trip and came across an encounter with the Snarly Yow. As he fired at the creature with his hunting rifle, the bullets merely passed through the body of the creature as if it occupied no space. As the Snarly Yow jumped towards him, it appeared as if none of his shots were making a dent into the creature of which caused him to turn around and run out of the forest as quick as he could move. To this day, many others report the same creature lurking around their property or in the forests nearby, preying on creatures too curious to back away from the shadowy figure roaming the area. Some believe it to potentially be a form of demonic dog known as a Hellhound whereas others believe it could be the malevolent spirit of a wolf from eons ago.

Number 4: The Demonic House Of Puerto Montt

The Carabineros are the militarized police force of the small South American country, Chile, of whom are trained with advanced techniques and provided the complete jurisdiction across the country to combat any illegal activities and forces that threaten the safety of the public; however, it appears that there are a few cases that even these Carabineros can not handle. Reports surfaced of a group of the militarized police claiming to have experienced a cluster of strange paranormal events that began transpiring in a home located in the Chilean southern city of Puerto Montt after responding to several calls for assistance from a family plagued by demonic activity.

When the military force arrived, they quickly noticed that the family had moved all of their mattresses outside, scattered across the lawn, as they were spending their nights sleeping outside. Sergeant Boris Olavarria then entered the house and claimed that a trowel located in the attic had flown at him during his inspection of the home. Another officer claimed to have been scratched and personally attacked when entering the home in an effort to investigate the claims of the Sergeant and to confirm the unexplainable paranormal activity. Shortly thereafter, the officer shouted for the demonic presence to leave the home in the hopes of conquering the demonic entity but was then thrown to the floor as his back was grazed with markings that appeared to be made from a large knife.

The other officers recorded the event with astonishment as it was impossible for the officer to have sustained such injuries as the officer was still wearing his bulletproof vest and there were no additional markings present on the vest. Over the course of a variety of different investigations, more powerful tactics were used by the entities against the officers attempting to better understand the events unfolding around them such as that of the demonic entity creating large amounts of smoke out of nowhere, lifting and throwing objects at the officers, as well as attacking a reporter of whom went into the home to investigate the claims made by the policemen.

This appeared to be one of the strongest pieces of evidence of a demonic presence and the investigation continued as the family was forced to remain in the home as they had nowhere else to go. Unfortunately, not much else is known of the investigation as efforts made by media to gather more information has been halted by the police force under efforts made by the Chilean government.

Number 5: Cabeca Satanica

Definitely the most unsettling urban legend by far is that of the Cabeca Satanica, also known as the Head of Satan or the Wandering Head. The Cabeca Satanica is a Brazilian demon or spirit that is described as having long, stringy black hair, bright glowing red eyes like that of a fire and high pitched tittering laugh that can pierce your eardrums.

Reports from locals vary widely on how the head is encountered. Some claim that it can only be encountered in the deeper jungles as it drops from the trees and attempts to latch onto those who pass by underneath whereas others claim the head can roll around until it finds someone to curse. If a person happens to be touched by the Cabeca Satanica, they will become cursed and soon develop a mysterious terrible sickness that will eventually lead to a fatal tragedy.

The origin of this story seems to also be shrouded in mystery as no one is really certain as to what exactly causes the presence of the head and after it touches a victim, it will mysteriously vanish and disappear without a trace, leading many who have encountered it to be nothing more than a strange dream or hallucination.

Others claim that as the head drops down from the trees, it can even begin floating and flying towards its target until it reaches them. Becoming a target of the Cabeca Satanic appears to not have a way to stop the curse as the head will not cease to touch the person it is wishing to curse and no known cure for the mysterious illness is believed to exist. The only possible explanation for getting the head to stop chasing you if you find yourself unfortunate enough to become one of its targets, is to instead force another person to touch it and take your curse for you which will then cause the Cabeca Satanica to disappear in a fit of laughter.

Ghosts From Around The World

It appears that, all around the world, there are strange stories and urban legends arising concerning the trapped ghosts and spirits of a person stuck in perpetual agony. These ghosts have ultimately made a name for themselves in the world of the paranormal and are often regarded as one of the most popular pieces of evidence when it comes to exposing the world of the paranormal. In this section, we will be going over six different ghosts from around the world and the legends that lead up to their creation.

Number 1: The Greenbrier Ghost

Although many might be well aware of the legends of strange monsters roaming the state of West Virginia, many are not aware of the existence of the urban legend involving the story of the Greenbrier Ghost. According to the rumors in the Greenbrier county of West Virginia, there were reports of a wife that had gone missing back in 1897, only for her body to be found at the foot of the stairs in her childhood home. It was originally believed that she had died due to natural causes but further evidence then pointed to signs of a struggle beforehand.

A few weeks later, the mother of the victim claimed to have encountered the angered spirit of the daughter that told her the true nature of her death. This then led to the court using the mother's testimony of the ghost to located the murdered nearby, a blacksmith that had entered the town as a drifter and held a mysterious past. After a further autopsy, it was revealed that the neck had been broken with finger markings made apparent after a few days of bruising to form. The man then confessed to the murder and was held and tried for the murder of the victim. Today, many believe that the ghost the mother had seen was indeed the ghost of the victim found at the bottom of the stairs and many others have claimed to have seen this manifestation since then, now referred to as the Greenbrier ghost.

Number 2: The Ghost of Longleat House

Lady Louisa Carteret of England was known during her time for dressing in nothing but grey and grey clothing. It is most likely due to this that the appearance of a grey dressed woman roaming the halls of the Longleat House have time and time again surfaced in reports made by visitors of the house. The legends go that the Lady was madly in love with her footman, of whom was described as being the most devout and loyal servant to have ever existed, of which sparked a jealous outrage from the husband. In a fit of rage, the husband had the servant killed and then buried underneath the house with not another word given on the matter.

Lady Carteret, at the time, was told that the servant ran away with a few precious jewels and had vowed never to return. Unwilling to believe the lie, the lady spent every day searching through the house looking in rooms of which she was forbidden to visit all across the massive estate in the hopes of finding the servant tied up or restrained against his will. It appears that her ghost is still searching for the servant to this day as many have often reported seeing the ghost speeding past them into different rooms at all times of the day. Additionally, the Longleat house is even known for being the site of one of the most compelling instances of a haunting caught on tape that still has many video experts pouring over its creation with extreme precision. It appears that not only is the footage genuine, but that the figure of the apparition matches that of Lady Louisa Carteret, a piece of evidence that has helped to keep the myths surrounding the house alive and well even in the modern day.

Number 3: The Crying Girl At King's Cross

After Investigations were held, it was revealed that on the 18th of November, back in 1987, an individual dropped a lit match onto the King's Cross Station escalator located in London, England, leading out to its main exit. This small match led to the development of a massive underground fire that completely destroyed the ticket office area, led to more than 30 people found burned alive and trapping more than a hundred other individuals underground. It is no surprise then that this terrible day led to the developments of one of the worst hauntings seen in the area. Every now and then people will report seeing a strange apparition of a young woman with long brown hair dressed casually in modern day jeans and a t shirt while crying hysterically.

Many have reported trying to console her or going up to talk to her only to see the apparition fade away and disappear before their very eyes. Although there is not much to correlate her to the tragic fate of that day back on November 18th, many believe that the ghost is a manifestation of a victim at the station that was left unrecognizable from the burns her body received. Interestingly enough, this also seems to match up with many other claims that people have reported in which they describe a smell of smoke or burning flesh when she appears. Maintenance workers have even reported hearing her sobs long after the station is at its lowest number of visitors with no one to be found at the empty platforms. The appearance of crying children are usually at the center of such tragic cases and this could very well mean that the crying girl at king's cross is evidence of a spirit still in the phases of crossing over to the other side.

Number 4: The Tale Of The Ironed Lady

The tale of La Planchada, also known as the Ironed Lady, is believed by many in Mexico as the source of strange ghostly nurse sightings across different hospitals in Mexico. According to witnesses, there appears to be the apparition of a nurse that will visit those gravely ill and tend to them before they pass away. The legend of the Ironed lady was first told in rumor as that of a hardworking nurse falling madly in love with a doctor that rejected her. After being rejected, she purposefully got gravely ill in the hopes of being cared for by the doctor that rejected her but passed away shortly thereafter in the hospital. To this day, the sight of a ghostly nurse is that of an omen, destined to take you to the other side due to your injuries or illnesses.

Number 5: The Story
Of Screaming Jenny

According to myths in the region of West Virginia, a terrible tale involving a caring woman and a tragic end seem to surface every year told by people who claimed to have come face to face with the ghost of Screaming Jenny. The story tells of a woman of whom never had much. She lived in a small storage shed located near the tracks of an old railroad that was rarely ever used. Often times, even though Jenny did not have much, she was known for giving what she could to those around her and even caring and tending to those sick or wounded.

One day, however, as she was eating her soup close to a fire in the shed, her gown caught aflame and she could not put it out. She quickly ran from her shed to the train station in the hopes that someone could help and crossed the tracks as her body soon engulfed in a fiery blaze. Her misfortune did not seem to end there; however, as the rarely used track was occupied by a fast moving train coming in without a stop which caused the train to slam into Jenny, ending her in an instant. It seems that according to the legend, her story does not end there. Every year, on the anniversary of her death, train conductors and other reputable sources claim they can see and hear the screaming of Jenny in her last moments right at the bend where she supposedly passed away.

Number 6: The Grey Flats Ghost

If you have ever been in the region of the Grey Flats forests near the town of Beckley West Virginia, then you will surely know what people mean when they refer to the place as eerie and haunted. According to the local legends, the most haunted part of the forest is located at an old farm right near the south end of the flats. Although people in the region believe an old mysterious murder to have occurred there, witness accounts of a group of friends encountering a strange creature seem to expand on the creepiness of the region. According to a group of friends that were hiking in the region a few years ago, as they approached the old farm on the south end of the forest, they noticed a strange figure in the distance that appeared to be a man wearing a long trench coat and a wide brimmed hat.

As they stood watching, the figure got much closer revealing to be a strange black shadowy figure with no depth other than its darkened silhouette. One of the friends began to panic and had what appeared to be an asthma attack and quickly got out of the area and carried their friend away from the creature. As they made some distance away, they realized their friend was not having an asthma attack but appeared to have had an unexplainable allergic reaction to the creature when it approached. Although the event could not be accurately explained, it seemed to share odd similarities with other myths and creatures in the region. The strange shadow creature then gained the moniker of the Grey Flats Ghost.

History of the Djinn

In all cultures and myths from around the world, there appear to be repeating themes of those discussing strange and malicious entities often referred to as demonic entities. Interestingly enough, it appears that the religion of Islam also speaks of these darker and malicious entities and refers to them as the People of the Fire or, more accurately, as the "Djinn". Although they do share a lot of the same characteristics of those of the demon, it appears that the Djinn are far more powerful and can even be tamed by a common man. In this section, we will be talking about the Djinn, the history behind them as well as strange and supernatural encounters of those of whom have seen the Djinn in modern times.

Number 1: Where Do The Djinn Come From?

According to the ancient scriptures seen throughout the Middle East, the Djinn are often referred to as the People of the Fire and seem to be as old as the universe itself. Scholars have noted that the word Djinn itself most likely comes from the arabic root word "Jann" to which roughly translates to mean "to hide" or "to conceal" which gives us a clue as to the nature of the Djinn of which were often regarded as creatures of whom would attempt to conceal themselves from man. The Quran then clarifies that the existence of the Djinn first came about during the act of the creation of the universe and that the Dfinn came into existence after being crafted from a smokeless fire, similar to that of electricity and much purer energy.

These stories, in fact, match that of the Judaism interpretation of the creation of Lucifer, of whom was also crafted from fire and not that of light similar to other angels. The Djinn were then described as being more accurately referred to as, the People of the Fire and that they would exist in a plane that rested slightly above ours but still within our world, slightly out of the reach of any of our natural senses. Additional information as to the origin and spreading of the Djinn get a little hazy thereafter but references are made of the Djinn assisting ruthless kings and rulers and even helping with the building and construction of many cities and places of immense power.

It is hard to refer to a Djinn as a demon, as the Qu-ran and other scriptures will often differentiate between the two, as the scripture specifies that a good Djinn is simply referred to as a Djinn but a bad and malicious Djinn is often just referred to as a demon. According to these scriptures, the Djinn are similar to man in that they possess the ability of free will and are even judged for their actions at the end of their lives.

Number 2: The Power of the Djinn

Given the fact that the Djinn are often described as being unable to be seen or sensed by our natural senses and constantly attempting to evade detection of all kind, it is no surprise then that the main focus of the power of the Djinn circles around its ability to take any form. It is believed that the Djinn have the ability to take the form of any animal or person and that they will often use these tactics to get away from someone pursuing them or to trick loved ones of an individual into doing something for them. The only way for someone to be certain of whether or not the creature is a Djinn is to look into its eyes.

According to legends, the Djinns' eyes are constantly blazing like a fire and that they can be seen in the eyes of any form that they take. Djinns also possess supernatural abilities such as that of possessing an individual to take control of their body, being able to predict the future and being able to perform superhuman feats that are otherwise unexplainable in the physical world such as speed, flying, vast intelligence, fluency in any language and a vast amount of unending skills. There are many references in different cultures in the region that often spoke of using the Djinn as an assistant in construction projects given their incredible supernatural abilities. Kings have claimed whole rivers had been carved out by hand over night by the creatures, others had temples built that were some of the largest man made creations ever seen, all attributed to the supernatural prowess of the Djinn. It is understandable then that given these tales that the west-ern interpretation of the Djinn referred to as genies tell the story of such creatures granting wishes.

In old Middle Eastern scriptures, it appears there were several cases in which evil and malevolent Djinn were trapped and bound and were then released by a man of whom stumbled across them. As a reward for being made free once again they would promise a favor for anything the man would want. Although they were incapable of granting wishes, their powers of shape-shifting, flight, super speed and super strength helped them to achieve next to anything a person asked them for, leading to the myths of the genie. Though these creatures could not age and could take any form they wished, it was made apparent in the Quran that the Djinn are, in fact, mortal and, in very rare cases, can be killed. Although it does not specify how a Djinn is killed or in what way they can be killed, mortality appears to be one of the main fears of the Djinn as they will almost always promise anything to be freed once they have been bound and restrained.

Number 3: Cultures That Reference The Djinn

Although many might believe that the Djinn are only referenced in the Islamic faith, the word and the reference to the creatures pop up all throughout early human history and even find themselves in amongst many scriptures of the world's most ancient religions and cultures. Beliefs in entities similar to that of the Djinn are often found all throughout Pre-Islamic Middle Eastern cultures, in fact. The Ancient Sumerian civilization, one of the oldest in existence, believed in the Pazuzu, of which had characteristics similar to the Djinn in that, though many might have referred to it as a demon, it had the ability to be both a malevolent or benevolent being and also possessed the ability to shapeshift. The Ancient Babylonians held the belief of a strange entity known as the Utukku in which might also have its origins similar to that of the Djinn.

The Utukku were described as being a class of demonic entities that haunted the remote wilderness, graveyards, mountains and the sea which are all the locations in which the Quran tells us that the Djinn reside. Not much is ever explained about the Utukku other than their disdain for human beings and their need to be hidden away from sight. Even the Judaist religion believes in entities similar to that of the Djinn, that are referred to as the Shedim. The Shedim are described as being supernatural creatures in early Jewish mythology and resemble the Islamic concept of the Djinn almost word for word.

Both are described as being invisible to the human eyes but often chasing physical desires. Both have the ability to be either benevolent or malevolent, and similar to the creation of the Djinn, the Shedim were created shortly after the angels and before the reign of man.

In fact, in the Talmud when regarding the legends of Solomon, the antagonist known as Asmodeus is given the title of being the king of the Djinn and the Shedim, signifying that both creatures are one and the same. The stories do not end there, however, as in the Buddhist religion, it was often referenced that the Buddha preached to humans and Djinn alike and even more references in scripture are made to the Djinn in the Christian religions and the Guanche mythologies.

Number 4: Modern Day Encounters With The Djinn

Even to this day, many locals in Iraq and other Middle Eastern countries give reports of Djinn and the usage of black magic. In fact, many people have been killed in public executions after having been charged with using black magic and attempting to summon Djinn or similar entities this past year. Today, many people of the Islamic faith are well-versed in the existence of the Djinn and will warn young ones or tourists not to trust people with fiery eyes and to be aware of any animals that might be following you wherever you go.

Number 5: Military Encounters With The Djinn

Definitely seen as one of the strangest reports of modern day encounters with the Djinn was a military encounter seen in Mosul, Iraq, back in June of 2003. An Iraqi soldier and other fighters were stationed at the second floor of a police department to assist with the attacks against the police between the locals and the law enforcement of the city. A lot of people were confused by the sudden attacks by the police and so one of the main purposes of the Iraqi army assisting with safety was to uncover the reasons as to why such disturbances were taking place. In one of the reports taken by an Iraqi military squad stationed for 24/7 surveillance, they claimed that they encountered several Djinn of whom were watching and patrolling the station.

The report details that they believed the individuals to be Djinn due to the fact that they had glowing red eyes and seemed completely unfazed by the bright surveillance lights used to blind passerbyers of whom attempted to get too close to the station at night. Shortly after the report was filed, the entire station was attacked and every soldier and police in the department were killed with no survivors. It then circulated that the Djinn were at the center of the attack and the majority of the disturbances were caused by the Djinn waging the plans of attack. After the report surfaced, the attacks stopped, with many locals claiming that the Djinn went back into hiding after they were discovered.

Are There Monsters Living Among Us?

In ancient scriptures and religions from around the world, we are embraced with the mythology of demonic entities and evil spirits that inhabit the Earth and walk among the cities of man. More accurately described as monsters, these beings are synonymous with concepts of evil and hatred, often being used as the literal depictions of disease, famine, suffering, pain and sin.

Today, unlike our ancestors in the times of ancient mythologies, we are not bombarded with the presence of such evils or demonic entities, in our day to day lives, nor are we aware of definitive proof of their existence. Many would argue that this is due to the fact that perhaps these entities no longer exist or never existed in the first place, but what if there is an alternative explanation? An explanation that helps to paint a better picture of our universe and allows us to better understand our place in it?

What if there are monsters living among us?
In 1999, at the University of Berkeley California, a cutting edge research scientist by the name of Dan Yang began working on her theories relative to the mind and capturing dreams. Her math was brilliant, understanding the complex data of the brain and being able to sift through its almost random firings and electrical impulses, she could recreate complex imagery from any mind she saw fit. Her goal was to be able to strap humans to a machine and to watch their dreams, an idea that sounded straight out of a Hollywood movie that was still yet to be made at the time.

Of course, the implications of such technology were profound, she soon found herself making another breakthrough, creepy and odd in its findings.

As the University funded her research, she was more than able to get approval for animal testing and was soon working with feline test subjects throughout her time in this endeavor. As she strapped cats to a machine that could gather data on brain waves and the electrical impulses throughout their brain, she began making strides in her mathematics and theory.

The idea was simple. She would force a cat to watch a movie for hours of the day and work to gather the data from the movie and the data the brain would provide and treat it as an encoded file. In theory, If the cat was watching the movie, she should be able to recreate, from the patterns of the felines brain, a mathematical system to convert brainwave and electrical impulse data back into a movie output.

Oddly enough, it worked.

She began being able to see what the cat was seeing and setting up an output from the converted data to an old box television monitor, she could see the images of the movie that the cat was capturing.

Dan Yang later clarified to a reporter as she said the following in an underground interview:

"*This is a digitized movie, we present this to the animal and we record the activity of the visual neurons and these electric signals, that we recorded from, will travel through these cables… so this is a digitized movie, this particular movie is a short clip from Indiana Jones, I think… the picture has a lot of random flickering and noise, that's probably the noise of the actual neurons because they sometimes fire spontaneous spikes, we consider those noise but maybe they reflect something else. Maybe the thoughts or something? but we can't distinguish that so when we use all of those [pieces of data] thinking that they represent visual information. This is the reconstruction that we come up with.*"

The creepiest part about all of this wasn't her success in being able to understand the visual information the cat was seeing, but the fact that for some strange reason, the cat saw human beings as other cats.

In each and every reconstruction that came forward from the output of the cat's visual neurons, every single human being that had been observed by the cat appeared to have a long snout, sunken eyes and the general appearance of a feline. In fact, we appeared to be bipedal cats similar in design to the Khajiit of Skyrim in the eyes of every single feline.

Though, theoretically, this makes sense.

Cat behavior analysts have found that, unlike every other species in the world, cats have been the only species to co-evolve alongside humans rather than becoming domesticated fully. This most likely appeared due to the fact that cats began living alongside humans as agriculture developed and humans and felines grew a symbiotic relationship relative to said agricultural developments.

This means that we benefited from having cats living among our fields because they killed vermin and cats benefited from living with us because they got to eat a lot of vermin that was produced by our organized crops.

In fact, we see many evolutionary changes among the housecat that has a developed sole purpose of manipulating the human population. Their purring is at a specific frequency that can heal their cells and human cells at a faster rate while also triggering hormones in the human brain that make them want to hold and nurture the purring feline. Their cries mimic the sounds of a human baby crying that also evolutionarily triggers a nurturing and feeding behavior. There are countless other evolutionary advantages that cats developed solely as the means of co-evolving alongside humans and have proven to be the only species to hold such developments.

One of these major developments is the inclusion of humans into their tribes.

Cats contain complex social hierarchies that work to create lasting relationships among their own kind, one of these complex social behaviors is the communication of language using their tails; however, at birth, cats are unable to use their tails or to learn this complex language so soon and so they come out of the womb crying and meowing towards their parents and their parents meow back to them. It isn't until cats grow and develop that they begin to understand these social practices and develop their own language, behaviors, personalities and accents.

However, humans never developed the ability to understand a cat's language, unless studying cat behaviors, this is why cats will meow to humans to communicate to them and display behavior towards humans similar to that of kittens. Cat behavior analysts began noticing that cats treated humans more as disabled adult cats rather than an outside species given their social hierarchies and developed behaviors. This is peculiar as cats don't do this with any other species except humans. This is what led to the evolutionary theory that since cats co-evolved with humans, it was evolutionary advantageous to treat humans as cats and include them in their tribes compared to any other animal species.

With Dan Yangs findings, this theory was solidified as it was realized that for some strange reason, cats are unable to see us in our true form and observe us literally and physically as fellow cats.

What if then there are monsters among us, walking in our streets, our cities and our homes, but we are, due to evolutionary advancements in co-evolution, completely unable to see them in their true form as they live among us?

What if there is an inhuman, a terribly frightening species, that our ancestors could see and observe that we lost the ability to see in its true form? Similar to how older cat species can view humans as humans but house cats view humans as fellow cats.

What if there was evidence of humans co-evolving and living alongside these monsters long enough and for benefit that we began to see them as human? In fact, this might very well be the case.

In every religious culture and ancient account around the world, they discuss the demons that lived alongside them. In scripture, after Cain killed Abel, it was said that his lineage mixed with the demons and generated offspring and heroes of old. In Ancient Greek mythology, this term of "Hero's of Old" is used when discussing demigods or humans that had special powers because they were half human and half something else.

In fact, up until the account of the Medieval Ages, there were still reports of demons being chained inside houses, sleeping with women and providing skills like teaching magic and granting powers of higher intelligence.

What if then, this is evidence of humans co-evolving among this inhuman species and slowly losing the ability to see a demon in its true form, as it was evolutionary advantageous to not be scared of them and to include them in our human tribes and social hierarchies?

How many times have you encountered someone that, for some strange reason, you could subconsciously feel the fear and terror and evil of the person standing next to you? That just by looking at them or standing near to them triggered some innate instinctual response to not trust them? Or to be weary of them?

Of course, this is purely subjective and debatable, but

given the advancements in theories among felines and their co-evolved history and inability to see humans in their true form, there is more evidence for the validity of this theory than there is against it. We aren't trying to say that this is factually true or 100 percent accurate as there may be a vital piece of the puzzle that we are missing in our theories but we are merely positing forward a theory and question that could possibly help you better understand your own subconscious mind and perhaps save your life if the feeling ever arises again.

Mysterious Ghost Ships

Ghost ships refer to the popularly coined term of a ship seemingly capable of running on its own as its entire crew has disappeared or abandoned the ship in an unknown haste. This story occurs time and time again on rescue missions of these ocean vessels where investigators discover a ship running completely smoothly on its own and the entire crew seems to have vanished without a trace. In this section, we will be going over a few of these specific cases and what could have possibly occurred to the missing crew of these abandoned ghost ships.

Number 1: MV Lyubov Orlova

Back in 1976, a Yugoslavian ice-strengthened Maria Yermolova-class cruise ship was built with the primary purpose to be used on cruises around the world that could venture near locations such as that of Antarctica. Unfortunately, the ship was decommissioned after the owner of the cruise ship racked up more than 250,000 dollars in debts that could not be paid and the entire crew of 51 people were left without a job. This eventually led to the ship sitting in a harbor for more than a decade before it was scheduled to be salvaged and destroyed given a lack of ownership, accrued debts and overwhelming charges for it being ported at the harbor. Before the ship could be destroyed, however, the line with the tugboat snapped and caused the boat to drift off to sea. Before the tugboat could reconnect the line, winds and waves picked up to more than 22 mph and 10 foot high walls of water soon pushed the boat away from the ship.

Before long, the abandoned Yugoslavian ice-strengthened cruise ship saw itself on the open ocean with no crew and nothing capable of stopping its force. Many believed that this was the end of the ship, however, and that it would soon sink. Oddly enough, this event occurred back in 2012 and there have still been reported sightings of the ship all around the world as it appears to be running strong even without a crew. Back in 2014, two years after this incident, proof was gathered that the ship was still active after a distress signal came from the ship that was located more than 700 miles off of the Kerry Coast. This has led researchers to believe that this ship had finally sunk at this point as the device is set to give off a distress signal upon hitting water. Still, strangely enough, reports of the ship without a crew sailing the ocean still seem to find their way in the modern day.

Number 2: MV Joyita

Back in 1955, the ship known as the Motor Vessel Joyita was found with a crew and passenger manifest of which had mysteriously disappeared in the South Pacific. According to detailed reports, at 5:00 A.M. on the 3rd of October, back in 1955, the Joyita left the Samoas Harbor en route to the Tokelau Islands only 270 miles away. She was carrying only 16 crew members and nine passengers including a government official, a doctor and a World War II surgeon ready to perform an amputation. This meant that for the crew, time was of the essence and yet, without sending a single distress signal, the boat never arrived at its scheduled location.

This led to officials launching a search party and rescue mission in order to better understand what happened, of which led to the boat being recovered more than 600 miles west of the Tokelau Islands. There had been no sign of the crew or passengers on board and more than four tons of the ship cargo was missing. When investigators looked further, they found that all the radios on the ship were tuned into the 2182 kHz radio signal, of which was the international marine radiotelephone distress channel.

Despite having been on the distress channel; however, no signal was received or transmitted. Although investigators believe that the ship had naturally formed a leak in its hull of which caused the entire crew to abandoned the ship, no effort was made by the crew to seek help and it appeared that the leak only would have began on the last few hours of the trip, making the predicament far more impossible to lead to the death of the entire crew and passengers. Alongside the missing cargo, many people believe the ship had possibly been attacked, however, evidence shows that the engines were still using full by the time the leak had poured into the floorboards of the engine which would have been close to the landing time of the ship. It appears that the mystery would never be uncovered and the crew and passengers were never heard from again.

Number 3: The Ryou-Un Maru

Similar to the story of the Motor Vessel Lyubov Orlova, the Ryou-Un Maru found itself sailing freely without a crew back in April of 2012, after the large earthquake and tsunami hit the Japanese coastline that caused the ship to become dislodged and drift out to sea. The vessel found itself sailing for over a year before the first few attempts at getting control back to be salvaged was made. Many were hopeful that the should could be recovered before sinking as to help cover costs accrued and to be used to assist with damages to the harbor caused by the earthquake in the region. Unfortunately, the ship had begun sailing too close to the Alaskan ports and the U.S. Coast Guard got involved. After deeming the ship too much of a hazard, before any further attempts could be made to salvage the vessel, the United states coast guard fired off several rounds of a MK 38 25 millimeter autocannon that quickly sank the ship to the bottom of the sea.

Number 4: The Recovery of the Kaz II

Known by many as one of the biggest Australian mysteries is the recovery of the Kaz II sailing yacht that has been given the name of "The Ghost Ship." After setting sail on the 15th of April, in 2007, with a three man crew, Derek Batten, Peter Tunstead and James Tunstead, the Kaz II would later be recovered on the 20th of April, merely 5 days later with a completely missing crew and no evidence of foul play. The authorities reported that the circumstances in which they found the found was incredibly strange. Everything appeared to be completely normal. Food and flatware was set up at the table as if the crew had been eating and stopped in the middle of their meal.

The laptop computer was set up and still on indicating that the battery life had yet to be drained and the boats engine was still running. No evidence of foul play was discovered which showed that there appeared to be no struggle of any kind on the ship but the cause for the disappearance of the crew could not be solved. Many regard the event as possibly supernatural or

extraterrestrial with cases of ghost ships and mysterious disappearances of a full crew happening all throughout history
similar to the case of the Mary Celeste and the missing U.S.S.
Submarine. As these are not isolated incidents, this could
very well mean that there is someone or something out there
causing these strange disappearances for reasons currently
unknown.

Number 5: The Lost Franklin Expedition Ship

Ghost stories and theories of potentially new uncovered diseases or monsters out in the vast expanse of unexplored territories arose after the mysterious disappearance
of the Franklin Expedition ship. In 1845, a British explorer
that went by the name Sir John Franklin began his expedition in the hopes of discovering a northwest passage through
the Canadian arctic. Although the voyage was incredibly
well-funded and the team was provided with more than
enough equipment and means to begin their journey, supplied with two ships and over 129 men, this did not prevent
the voyage from becoming a terrifying tragedy.

Sir John Franklin and his crew would completely
vanish from the face of the Earth and never be heard from
again after starting their hopeful endeavor. For decades the
circumstances surrounding the event remained a mystery.
In 1859, a group of explorers discovered two notes that had
seemingly hinted at the fate of the crewmen that were dated approximately a year apart. The first note had detailed
that the ships had become trapped in the ice and the crew
planned to wait out the winter before continuing their journey which remained filled with tones of an upbeat attitude
and hopeful promises.

The second note however took a dramatic turn. The
note reported that while the ships had continued to remain
trapped during the year, the crew of the two ships began
experiencing an unusually high mortality rate from an unknown cause. The note detailed that Sir John Franklin had
died under mysterious circumstances and the remaining
crew, that the note referred to as survivors, would attempt to

walk south to safety against whatever appeared to be responsible for their mortality rate. None of the crewman were found alive and the local Inuit population reported finding human bones with strange markings that made it appear as if whoever they found was eaten alive. No further evidence was uncovered and the full story of what had occurred remained a mystery.

This would change in 2014, however, as it was announced by then Canadian Prime Minister, Stephen Harper, that one of the ships had been recovered. This finding will likely hold clues about the exact fate of the expedition but has yet to be investigated fully. Oddly enough the second ship has yet to be found but there is no doubt that it will be uncovered soon enough. Unfortunately, further information regarding the recovered ship has not yet been made available to the general public.

People That Are Known Reincarnations

From the oldest of times across the vast expanse of human history, themes of multiple incarnations of an immortal soul revisiting the planet or across the expanse of the universe has been argued and entertained across cultures, religions and philosophical debates. The idea of an everlasting soul imparting itself in multiple iterations of life came to be widely known and referred to as the act of reincarnation, and though it is not a very popular belief, evidence for the event seems to be completely overwhelming. In this section, we will be visiting 5 people who are believed to be reincarnations of their former selves and have the overwhelming evidence to back up the claims.

Number 1: Bruce Whittier And The Recovered Clock

It is often the case that with supposed claims of reincarnation, many individuals claiming to have lived past lives will only making claims that are impossible to validate or numerous and vague in nature. This was not the case with Bruce Whittier. From a very early age, Bruce had terrifying nightmares and dreams that would often leave him feeling panicked and restless. To help solve the problems of his subconscious, Mr. Whittier later in his life began to record his dreams and began to recall events that had occurred in a past life. He believed that he was the reincarnation of a Dutch Jewish man that went by the name of Stefan Horowitz and had met the grave misfortune of being sent to Auschwitz, a Nazi death camp that operated during World War II.

Interestingly enough, Bruce Whittier had recurring dreams about a family heirloom that he could describe and draw in vivid detail. The heirloom appeared to be an antique clock with very specific designs and insignias that he had believed belong to him in his past life. After following a trail left behind by his past experiences, Mr. Whittier traced the location of the clock to an antique shop he had often seen in his dreams. As he and his family went to the shop, they found an antique clock in the stores window matching the drawings that Mr. Whittier had often scribbled down in an attempt to record his dreams. After entering the store and talking with the owner of the shop, the dealer had told them that the previous owner of the clock who had sold the heirloom was a retired German major in the Netherlands, corroborating Bruce's stories and memories of the stolen artifact. This only worked to convince Mr. Whittier and his family that he had indeed really lived as the Dutch Jew, Stefan Horowitz, in a past life.

Number 2: The Strange Case Of Imad Elawar

The first two words that came from the child's mouth were the names "Jamileh" and "Mahmoud", as reported by the parents and their fascination with the claims of their son. This would later go on to be referred to as the strange case of Imad Elawar, as a young boy, born in Lebanon, began speaking in detail about his past life in the nearby village. As the boy grew older, his recollection grew. When he was two years old and had an encountered a stranger from the nearby village, he stopped the stranger in the street and told him that he recognized him as a neighbor from his past life. When the stranger inquired additional information from Imad, the boy then began reciting accurate facts and details from the stranger's life.

Further claims from the child were made that led to a full on investigation by a man named Dr. Ian Stevenson. Dr. Stevenson then catalogued over 55 claims made by Imad and worked to validate them in the nearby village. The doctor then took the family and the young boy to the area that the boy had described in vivid detail, which led to even more startling discoveries. Imad and his family confirmed 51 out of the 55 claims Dr. Ian Stevenson had recorded. Imad even encountered an older man known as Mahmoud that he recognized as his uncle in a previous life and another person named Jamileh who was his mistress in a previous life. Not only were his claims confirmed as accurate but additional memories soon poured out of the child, being able to recall rooms, a hidden gun and other facts about the life of his past self.

Number 3: The Dalai Lama

Stretching back to now almost 14 incarnations, the Dalai Lama is believed to be, by the Tibetan people, a ruler that has the incredible ability to not only reincarnate, but to be able to choose the next form he will reincarnate into and be found as. Though many believe this to have been an old political move to selecting a new ruler, evidence of the Dalai Lama's reincarnation is profound, as an event and strict guidelines are provided to finding the newly reincarnated Lama in the times of need.

It was told that when the 14th Dalai Lama was found, the priests had visions of the location of the child that would eventually grow up to be the new heir to the Tibetan way of life. Additional details had been provided by the 13th Lama before his passing, of which region to search for his new reincarnated self. It was said that as the priests began their four year journey, they had stumbled upon the house and region the previous Lama had foretold and a young child approached them already aware of who they were and why they were there.

Further tests to prove the reincarnation was done, providing the child with a collection of toys and items. The 14th Lama then chose all of the toys and items that had belonged to the previous Lama with exact intent and recognition. If this is not enough evidence for the skeptics of reincarnation, then looking deeper into the past shows this same process occurring each time the Lama was found and personalities and behaviors of each new Lama seem to mimic the last.

Given visions of the future, the 14th Lama has provided new insight to his 15th form and said that his time might soon be coming. He believes that his next form will be that of a woman and that she will be found outside of the Asian territories. He also believes that upon his death, the Chinese government will attempt to input their own fraudulent Dalai Lama that should not be trusted as he will only work to systematically destroy Tibet and give it to Chinese rule. When asked about the reasoning of his new form, the 14th Lama merely stated that the body of the Lama is not important and is only selected if it helps the influence of the Lama and his teachings, believing that a new female form will help him to provide greater influence and power than his current form provides.

Number 4: The Account
Of James Leininger

From birth, James Leininger was often troubled by recurring nightmares and insomnia. As he grew up, his parents began noticing odd behavior that they could not quite understand. James, for some unknown reason, had an absolute fascination with toy airplanes. In fact, toy airplanes were the only toys he would play with and would often have closer attachments to older models of fighter planes. As he began learning how to speak, James would often spend his time talking about flying airplanes, the weapons attached to certain model fighter planes and often about a terrifying accident that he was in with his plane.

At three years old, James Leininger began showing even more strange information relative to airplanes to his mother, describing the plan drop tank of a fighter plane and even being able to perform pre-flight checks out loud during his play time with his toys. He would often give recounts after his nightmares saying that the middle of his engine was hit and that he was killed at Iwo Jima.

After further investigation from the father, the boy would later recall an experience he had been through in a previous life. Giving specific details of taking off from a ship called the Natoma with a co-pilot by the name of Jack Larson. Records found by the father would later show that there was indeed a military aircraft carrier referred to as the Natoma and co-pilots Jack Larson and a man by the name of James jr. were scheduled to take a flight together before being downed after a strike over Iwo Jima.

Number 5: Dorothy Eady

Regarded as one of the most compelling cases of modern day reincarnation, Dorothy Eady was a London born woman who worked to solve Ancient Egyptian mysteries and secrets and was regarded as a legitimate resource used by Egyptologists and famed archaeologists around the world. Dorothy Eady, born in London in 1904 made the claim that she was the living reincarnation of Om Seti, a high priestess selected from birth to be the keeper of the Abydos Temple of Seti.

What is so compelling of her account was reported that, at birth, Dorothy Eady could fluently speak and read the Egyptian language. This was more than odd given the fact that the Egyptian language had long since been extinct and no one currently alive was aware of how it sounded. Even those of whom had cracked the code behind the language and the Hieroglyphics were uncertain of exactly how the semantics and pronunciations of certain words were handled; that was until Dorothy Eady systematically taught and explained the language in vast detail that worked to confirm a lot of long standing theories as well as filling in old holes and mysteries.

Egyptologists would even later go on to prove the legitimacy of Dorothy Eady's fluency in Egyptian after they began studying neighboring native languages that arose and evolved from Egyptian in the area and found their slang and accents to directly mimic certain sounds, words and pronunciations by Dorothy Eady. This wasn't the height of her accomplishments, however, as she would later go on to help uncover many locations of Ancient Egyptian sites buried beneath sand, discover secret chambers and assist with the recovery of long forgotten and hidden Ancient Egyptian artifacts. In 1979, the New York Times wrote a piece on Dorothy Eady that regarded her as "*The western world's most intriguing and convincing modern case histories of reincarnation.*"

Pieces of Cursed Jewelry

Ancient Egyptians used to believe that envy itself could be used as a curse to destroy a person's life. In fact, they believed envy to be so dangerous that it could create such a powerful form of toxicity that only magical pendants and amulets could absorb this evil and thus prevent it from reaching with power over their lives. Of course, with this superstition in mind, it is not entirely impossible to believe that the jewels used by the rich and extravagant could absorb these curses similar to that of the ancient amulets used by the Egyptian culture and then become, themselves, cursed items. In this section, we will be covering two pieces of cursed jewelry so dangerous, it has driven their owners to madness or to death.

Number 1: The Black Orlov Diamond

Suicide is often described as a virus that could cause a string of further suicides of loved ones of the deceased and so is often referred to as an epidemic. This could not be more true in the case of The Black Orlov Diamond.

Rumored to have originally been a precious gem placed inside the Eye of Brahma from an Indian sculpture located in a secluded Hindu Temple, this diamond was stolen by a Jesuit Monk that had worked at said temple and went on to sell the diamond for a tremendous amount of money. It was this action that supposedly caused the diamond to become cursed and led to a series of suicides that worked as a virus to spread amongst others.

The original diamond dealer, of whom had purchased the Black Orlov Diamond from the Jesuit Monk, wrote extensively of his growing paranoia's and his depressive state being made worse by the piece of jewelry, stating that the diamond began encompassing his thoughts at nearly all times. He then took the diamond with him on his journey to the United States where, overcome by the curse of this diamond, went atop a skyscraper and jumped off.

The diamond was mysteriously missing until it resurfaced almost ten years later in the possession of a beautiful Russian princess, Leonila, that, after gaining possession of the diamond from unknown sources, began complaining of terrible head-aches and dreams that only worsened her mental state. It didn't take long before the Russian princess, herself, also jumped to her death.

Shortly after this, the diamond was then given pos-session to Nadia Orlov, another Russian princess of which the diamond would later be named after. Similar to all its previous owners, Nadia began complaining of mental illness and quickly deteriorated shortly after gaining possession of the diamond. Unsurprising to most, this would lead Nadia to jump to her suicide shortly after and another string of sui-cides from loved ones to follow her untimely death.

It wasn't until a man by the name of Charles Winson gained ownership of the diamond that the curse was broken. He originally was a skeptic of this diamond and wished to own it due to its incredible level of infamy. His tune quick-ly changed, however, as after gaining possess of the piece of jewelry, he began feeling as if he was being driven to insanity as the diamond encompassed his every thoughts and fueled a depressive state. Understanding the curse and his soon to be fate, Mr. Winson quickly worked to defeat the curse of the diamond by having it broken up into many separate pieces and scattered in different sets of bands and jewelry. It wasn't until this was completed in fruiting that Mr. Winson felt the curse lift and returned to normalcy.

Number 2: The Destiny Ring

In 1920, a Hollywood actor named Rudolph Valentino had become an incredibly popular celebrity during the height of the roaring twenties and had more than enough spending money in his pocket to pick out any piece of jewelry he so desired. He soon found, looking through the window of an antique shop in San Francisco, a ring that had a silver band and a semi-precious gem that had immediately overcome his senses and caused him to rush into the store and ask the shopkeeper for its price.

Strangely enough, the shopkeeper refused to sell Mr. Valentino the ring and explained to the celebrity that the ring is a cursed piece of jewelry that would only bring terri-ble misfortune to its wearer. The shopkeeper then further explained that this ring was called the Destiny Ring and had the ability to create terrible envy in the eyes of everyone around Mr. Valentino if he wore it and that the only reason he left it in the store window is because it helped to attract a tremendous amount of customers to the store.

Despite hearing this warning, Mr. Valentino begged the shopkeeper to forget about a stupid curse and attempted to bribe him with a substantial amount of money that far exceeded the value of the ring just to purchase the fine piece of jewelry he desired. After hours of negotiating and begging, the shopkeeper reluctantly sold the ring to Mr. Valentino while also heeding a terrible warning.

Soon after wearing the ring, Mr. Valentino had become gravely ill with bleeding ulcers and, though he had soon overcome this illness while attempting to film another movie, the damage done to the lining of his stomach was so extensive that it led it massive infections after the surgery that led to his death. Mr. Valentino died wearing the ring.

Taken from his dead body, his then lover at the time, Pola Negri, of whom was a popular actress and sex symbol across Hollywood, took ownership and possession of the piece of jewelry and quickly wore the Destiny Ring after eyeing the piece for some time.

Soon thereafter, Pola Negri also had become deathly ill and due to her sickness, killed her career in the process. Seeing the ring as a curse and believing what Mr. Valentino had been told by the anxious shopkeeper, she quickly gave the ring away to a young, up and coming singer who reminded her of Mr. Valentino called Russ Colombo. After giving away the Destiny Ring to Mr. Colombo, Pola Negri soon recovered and believed herself to be freed from this curse. Mr. Colombo himself, however, would go on to pass away less than a week later after being fatally wounded in a shooting accident.

After Colombo's passing, the ring was taken by Russ's friend that went by the name Mr. Joe Casino. Knowing about the fate of the previous owners and believing the curse to be legitimate, Mr. Casino originally refused to touch or wear the ring and quickly put it inside a glass case to prevent it from hurting others. This glass case didn't help to stop his envy, however, and the ring quickly became a piece worn by Mr. Casino after finding it unbearable to look at the ring and to not wear it proudly.

Only a week later, Mr. Casino would be struck dead of which was resulted due to a fatal hit from a truck that had run him over as he was crossing the street.

Joe Casino's brother, Del Casino, then inherited the ring and, blaming the cursed ring for his brother's death, immediately placed it inside a sealed safe never to be seen or heard from again, hoping this containment would prevent it from being seen and targeted by anyone's envy craving to own the piece of jewelry for the foreseeable future.

This wouldn't be the end of this ring's series of misfortunes though, as a burglar by the name of James Willis had broken into the home of Del Casino and began stealing precious items from the house. It wasn't until Mr. Willis had broken into the safe containing the cursed ring that he had tripped the silent alarm that alerted the police to his presence. When law enforcement arrived on the scene, they immediately shot and killed Mr. Willis only to find the ring in his pocket and, also believing the stories of the curse, quickly placed it back inside the safe.

Believing the ring to be responsible for this terrible tragedy, Del Casino then moved the piece of jewelry to another safe and told no one of its location, in the hopes of preventing envious thieves from taking action to steal the ring once more.

It wasn't until years later, when director Edward Small had discovered of the legends of this cursed ring when hoping to make a movie about the life of Mr. Valentino that he retrieved the ring to be used as a centerpiece of the film. He then gave this ring to an unknown actor named James Dunn that was to portray Mr. Valentino in the film, but soon led to tragedy as no more than two weeks later, James Dunn had died from a mysterious blood disease that seemingly had no origin.

After being given the ring back, Del Casino remained in possession of the ring until his death years later that led to his possessions being moved to a bank vault. Of course, one of these possessions was the cursed ring itself.

The bank would then be the victim of a series of robberies, fires, and worker strikes that would then build up to uncovering the rings sudden disappearance as it was suspected an employee of the bank themselves had taken the ring during the working day. After the disappearance of the ring, the series of misfortunes for the bank ended. The whereabouts of the Destiny Ring are unknown to this day.

An interesting piece of information recovered while researching this topic allowed us to discover that though there are few depictions and images of the ring that exist, the ring was rumored to appear as that of a tiger's eye. Similar in design to the evil eye of Egyptian lore, the Destiny Ring seemed like a perfect candidate to absorb the envious attitudes of others and harbor this curse.

Reported Encounters
Of Shadow-like Entities

Below are the real witness accounts of stories sent in concerning encounters with a Shadow Person. A Shadow Person, also known as a shadow figure, shadow being or black mass is the perception of a patch of shadow as a living, humanoid figure, particularly believed to be paranormal or supernatural entity and believed to be the presence of a specific shadow spirit of darker entity. A number of religions, myths and legends from around the world describe shadowy spiritual beings or supernatural entities such as shades of the underworld, which helps to provide evidence that various shadowy creatures have long been a staple of folklore and ghost stories. Today, we will be going over real life horror stories and witness accounts of encounters with these shadow people and their dark nature.

Number 1: A Man Under The House

Back when I was around 12, my family and I used to live in this old house that had been around since the early 1900's, the house was somewhere between 100 to 106 years old, according to the previous owners that we had purchased the house from. At the time, I never really believed the house was haunted but I was aware of the trope that many old homes probably had something bad happen in them and that because of that, the house most likely had some evil energy attached to the place to some degree. In all honesty, for the majority of our time living there, which spanned over 6-7 years, nothing really outrageous happened except for maybe a handful of different instances. Strange knock on the door to the bedrooms when we were trying to sleep, a book flying off the shelf across the room and one instance when the cats refused to enter the house and when we would try to bring them in, they would begin to panic badly.

None of that really even compared to this one weird instance that had us questioning whether or not the home we were living in was safe. There was this one time that we had to send a plumber underneath the house to inspect some old pipes that were probably long overdue of being replaced. The house was elevated roughly 8 feet above the ground so though there was an open space to get underneath the home, it was nothing more than wooden stilts on top of bare ground supporting the house and you would have to crawl underneath the home just to see the piping going in.

The wooden stilts of the house were not visible since the entire house had wooden panelling wrapped around it. So though there was this large space that you could most likely stand up in, you had to enter the house from the backyard and crawl in from underneath the porch stairs to get in. Because of the wooden side paneling all around the house, the space underneath was usually completely pitch black and so plenty of us were usually too terrified to enter because of more mundane reasons such as encountering a possum, a hive of cockroaches or stepping on old rusty nails. Before going in, the plumber said he would only be going down for a quick inspection. It was the middle of the day so I'm sure he had many other appointments to get to at other houses immediately after ours.

When he crawled into the space under the house through the underside of the porch stairs, he began shouting back to us that his flashlight did not seem to be working properly. He crawled back out and seemed a little more quiet than usual. As he tapped his flashlight and saw the light coming out, he stared at it a little while and then looked at us and said "It's weird, it's almost like I can't see the light down there. Like something is absorbing my flashlight's light." He waited awhile as if to see our reactions and then crawled back in. This time, he didn't shout anything back but quickly came out again.

He was breathing hard and his eyes were really big as if he had been panicking. When he came out he said "I know this is going to sound crazy, but I think there's someone down there." He quickly grabbed the board that we usually placed to board up the area and blocked the hole. We called the cops and told them that there was some man under our home. When the cops came and inspected, they didn't find anyone and the plumber claimed to have seen a large black shadowy mass come at him and push him. It was after that incident that we started hearing strange knocking throughout the house as if someone was rapping their knuckles against wood. The knocking didn't come from the doors this time though, it came from underneath the house.

Number 2: The Monster At The Foot of My Bed

My son would often come into me and my wife's room screaming that he had seen a monster down at the foot of his bed. Of course, as a parent, even if you don't believe in what was happening or you knew that it was nothing than a nightmare, you still need to be sensitive approaching such topics with your kids. Some nights I would get up and go to his room with him and sit in the room until he fell back to sleep, other nights I would just tell him to sleep with us because I would find that I was too tired to get up. We had always believed that our son was experiencing nothing more than nightmares that he was incapable of separating from waking up in fear and what he saw in the dream, so we never really pursued it any further and we would just help him to feel safe when he was scared. It really didn't change until this one night where I had went to bed a little later than usual.

My wife and I usually worked all day from 4 am and so when we got home, did chores and made dinner, we would usually go to bed shortly after eating. This meant that 7 or 8 pm was usually our collective bedtime because by the time the clock started rolling around that time, we couldn't keep our eyes open any longer. There was this one day where I didn't go to work and I slept in because I was sick really bad with the flu. By the time it was time to pick up our son from school, I was still barely getting out of bed which threw my entire sleeping schedule all out of whack. When 8:00 P.M. rolled by, my son and I were still up watching cartoons and my wife was fast asleep.

At around 10:00 P.M, my son told me that this was usually the time when the shadow man came out and that he wouldn't be too happy if we were still watching T.V. which seemed really odd to me and actually gave me the creeps. I figured that maybe my son was just getting ready for bed and wanted to go to sleep, though I don't think he's ever wanted to go to sleep in his life and we still stayed up another hour watching some old superhero cartoon.

When we get to his bedroom, he quickly ran to his bed and pulled the covers over him without saying anything to me as if he was scared of this shadow man. I wanted to ask him about it but figured that bringing it up would only make the situation worse so I just went to go lay down with my wife.

As I laid down and began starting to fall asleep, suddenly I heard this scream coming in through the door which startled me. I sat up and saw that the door to our room was wide open and half expected to see my son coming in, believing that maybe he opened the door. After a moments silence, I heard my son running down the hallway into the room which honestly probably scared me even more than the scream. He was crying terribly which woke up my wife. When I asked him what was wrong and what happened he said "Did you hear him? He came into my room screaming at me and then he came into your room and screamed at you. I told you we were going to make him mad." Ever since then, whenever our son said he would see the shadow man. I believed him.

Number 3: The Haunted Forests Of West Virginia

Every year, my friends and I would meet up and go on a hike together to just hang out, have some fun and catch up with what's usually going on in our lives.

If you have ever hiked to the Grey Flats woods located near the small town of Beckley, West Virginia, then you know how eerie those woods can be even during the middle of the day. Despite how creep the grey flats may be; however, there's no more eerie a place in all the flats than the of the old farm beyond the south end of the flats forest.

There the Old Farm Trail meets the South Grey Flats Trail in a patch of twisted thorns and overgrown brambles. That patch of bramble and the decrepit old oaks and maples that shade it are all that is left of an old farm, the ruins of which have been there as long as anyone can remember, though there is little to be found but old foundation stones. Hikers and bikers on the trail have long told strange tales of a haunting there, but I did not put much stock in those local tales until a few years ago when my friends and I actually saw something that none of us can explain. It was nearly dusk in late October as we found the area to be both cold and drizzly, and though that made seeing difficult, what we saw was plainly visible.

At the point on the Grey Flats Trail where trees move in close together, we saw a black figure in what can only be described as a long coat and a broad-rimmed hat. Though man-shaped, it had no obvious depth as no light fell upon it. It was completely black. And rather than moving like a normal person, it moved without walking. And it moved to the side, away from us up through the trees away from the road toward what might have been the farmhouse. And though the rocky ground rose, the figure did not. It appeared to move into the earth.

As soon as it disappeared into the ground, my friend Becky began to get sick. She held her hands over her stomach and bent down and began to let out of kind of a long sob. We asked her if she was alright and she shook her head yes, that she just wanted to go home, so we grabbed her by the arms and went back out toward Ship Rock. Just as we were getting ready to turn onto the old farm trail we looked back and saw the shape again. It appeared to be emerging from the ground and heading down toward where the old strip mines were.

I have no explanation for what we saw. I have heard that someone was murdered near the farm many years ago, but after looking into the rumors, I found that I can not find anything to confirm that. This is the only time I have ever had anything that I could describe as being a supernatural experience. I have been past the site many time since and have never seen anything, though I don't linger long waiting to encounter it once again.

Number 4: Breaking Down At The Side of The Road

When I was real small, I would often see this shadow person wearing what I could only describe as a large cowboy hat that would often enter my room and just stare at me from the doorway. This happened so often that I started getting used to it and not really being all too bothered by it. My trick was to just keep my eyes closed throughout the night even if I heard the door begin to creak open. Whenever I would try to tell anyone about it, they just thought I was talking about a nightmare or sleep paralysis and would tell me that it was nothing and that it's just something that would run in the family. Since I had uncles and grandparents tell me this, I just started to believe them and believed that I was suffering from sleep paralysis almost every single night and since it would happen as I would get ready to go to bed or in the middle of the night, I figured it made more sense than any other explanation available.

When I was in my 30's I would have a long late commute through the night that would take me roughly an hour or some just to drive home through the mountains. I never really minded the drive all too much because the scenery was so inviting and I could find that with the right kind of music and the right kind of weather, it was a sort of meditative experience. As I was driving, my car seemed to hit a bump and my engine shut off suddenly which forced me to pull over to the side of the road and turn on my emergency lights. My phone had died and I had no way of charging it, even if I did, I was so far out in the mountains that there was no way I could possibly get a signal even if I tried.

I tried a few times to turn the engine up but I couldn't hear a click or anything. As I got out of the car to pop the hood, I noticed a large black mass coming out of the forest around me. At first I thought it was a bunch of deer crossing so I quickly ran in the car so that I wouldn't be in the way. I then began to see what appeared to be hundreds of shadow people coming out from the greenery around me and walking through like a horde of zombies. I closed my eyes and put my head down and began praying as softly as I could until I thought they were gone.

Without even opening my eyes, I began turning my car keys praying for my engine to ignite. After a few turns it roared to life and I opened my eyes to leave. When I opened them, I saw this thin shadowy figure standing in front of my car staring at me with these deep red eyes which caused me to panic and run it over. As my car drove at the figure, he went through the car and passed through me like nothing. Almost caused me to crash. I raced home, turned on all the lights and couldn't fall asleep until the next morning. Ever since then, I haven't seen a single shadow person. But I still keep my eyes closed tight when I wake up in the middle of the night.

Number 5: Security Footage

I used to work as a store manager for this business owner back in my hometown who owned two of the top selling retail stores in the area that usually attracted a good amount of people all throughout the day. Top selling really did not mean much given that we lived in a small town in a fairly deserted area but this did mean that there were plenty of jealous people all throughout the town that wanted to break in and see what they could get, including other business owners that wanted nothing more than to ruin the store.

Luckily for us, the owner had pretty state of the art safety measures, supplied the employees with bear spray, and even included a gun in the back safe in case it was ever needed that was only accessed by myself and the other store manager for the neighboring location. The security equipment consisted of sensors on the windows, doors, roof, walls and even the floor to make sure nothing was in the store. All around the store were several cameras that were in high definition and recorded in night vision when things got too dark and would store the footage raw for up to 30 days, highlighting anything that activated the cameras sensors.

There was this one night I was home and I get a call from the store owner who was on his way down to the store calling me to ask if there was anyone entering the store at the time. It was roughly 11 pm at the time so I said no and asked if everything was okay. He then told me he was gonna call the cops and that I should check the footage from the security cameras to see what's going. The cameras were connected to the wifi so as long as you had the account information, you could access them from your phone, which is what I did.

On the footage, live as I was watching it, there was this shadow person walking around the store that did not activate any of the sensors from the security alarm. Although the camera picked up its movements, it was only due to the change in light that caused the pixels to differ enough for the cameras to alert that something was in the store. After awhile, I see the cops pull up to the store and then the store owner pull up. The store owner began talking to the cops and giving them the keys to the store to have them go on, at this point the figure inside began running towards the window at them. It looked almost as if it split into multiple different shadowy figures and rushed the cop car.

The cop quickly pulled out his flashlight and began waving it around as the store owner ran back to his car and turned the lights on. When the lights came on from the car, it looked as if the shadowy figures disappeared. The store owner never exited the car but seemed as if he was talking to the cop through the window before they both pulled out and left without checking the store. That next day, I asked the store owner what happened and that I saw the footage. He refused to talk to me about it and said that he would be sure to remove the footage so that no one asked anymore questions. Never really understood what I saw or what happened but after finding out about attacks from shadow people from random personal stories on the internet, I'm convinced that that was what occurred that night.

The Truth About
The Aokigahara Forest

Known by its more popular alternative name, the Aokigahara Forest is most commonly called, by people around the world, the Suicide forest. This is due, in part, to the large amounts of suicides that have occurred in the region as people will travel great distances just to silently disappear and end their lives while experiencing the beautiful scenery of the world around them. However, the suicides are not the height of the weird and unexplainable phenomena that occur inside the suicide forest. In this section, we will be going over, 5 creepy facts about the Aokigahara Forest.

Number 1: Sound Refuses to Travel

It is entirely unclear what the specific cause of this strange occurrence is but for some odd reason still being worked on and researched today, the forest actively deafens the sounds made inside it. It is a common occurrence for individuals to walk right past each other without hearing any noise or being aware of the presence of the individuals beside them due to sound becoming strangely muffled when entering inside the forest. A hypothesis has been posited forward that believes the porous volcanic rock, of which makes of the majority of the land and geographical features in that area, work to absorb any sounds made inside the forest. In essence, this porous volcanic rock begins acting similar to that of a natural acoustic treatment and prevents sounds from traveling any kind of distance.

The physics for this claim are still in question and, to this day, still remains widely debated amongst researchers of the area. There are many others who believe that the muffling powers of the forest could be due to the unnatural growth of the trees, plants and forest around them that begin to work to naturally muffle sounds traveling beneath the canopy of the trees in the forest but tests are inconclusive and many other researchers remain skeptical of this hypothesis. There is still a wide debate for why this strange phenomena occurs, but one thing that every person who visits the region can agree on is that it is a rather peculiar behavior of the forest not seen elsewhere and a rather creepy one.

Number 2: This Forest Is Darker and Denser

Adding onto the strange phenomena that occur in the Aokigahara Forest, the forest is also incredibly darker and denser than other forests nearby in that general region. In fact, the forest is so dangerous and threatening due to these factors, even during the middle of the day, that well-experienced hikers and travelers have had to use different forms of colored tapes, plastics, bands and markings just to be able to navigate through the forest without getting lost inside its dense growth and dramatically darkened interior. Most even reporting that it is nearly impossible to tell night from day in certain denser regions of the forest due to the canopy of the trees above them blocking out any form of light.

This has contributed to the belief that perhaps not all bodies found inside the forest were acts of suicide, but rather more accurately, of hikers and travelers getting lost inside the forest and eventually dying of exhaustion. There is evidence to support this theory as most bodies that are recovered are so decayed and rotted that it is nearly impossible to tell the immediate cause of death.

There are also strange reports of people being unable to see a person standing next to them and have to hold hands just to make sure not to lose each other. It becomes incredibly more terrifying when you take into account additional witness reports that talk about strange lights moving through the forest similar in design to orbs.

Number 3: Compasses Refuse to Work

A fear that rests in the minds of even the most experienced hikers and travelers is the possibility of a broken compass that can work to lead said hiker only further into deeper isolation. This is more than just a fear in the minds of visitors of the Aokigahara Forest however as strange occurrences have been happening and reported by many who find themselves lost in the dense undergrowth of the forest.

Though continually denied by officials and "investigators", there has been a tremendous amount of accounts of individuals claiming that their compass will begin to act erratically and become broken while inside the Aokigahara Forest, only for the compass to return to normal once outside of the denser regions of the forest.

Some posit the theory that due to the strong electromagnetic presences of the volcanic rock that makes up the area, it is highly plausible that a compass could begin picking up this sudden interference and cease to work while inside the forest. This theory had proven to be inconclusive, however, as experts tested electromagnetic equipment and found the volcanic rock to be unable to affect compasses or devices of any kind.

Due to this finding, paranormal experts posit a more reliable theory. In the areas that witnesses report these strange interferences, it is found that there are similar groupings of reports from people that visit those specific areas. These specific areas also coincidentally have a high amount of reports relative to ghost sightings and supernatural occurrences by unrelated parties passing through the area at different times.

Paranormal experts believe that the changes in the electromagnetic energies of the area could be caused by the presence of spirits as they begin to manifest in the region. Which means that if your compass begins to malfunction, it is most likely because something is following you.

Number 4: Massive Amounts Of Suicides

Though many might not be surprised by this creepy fact, there are such a massive amount of suicides in the forest, that it is possibly the highest place of total suicides in the world. In previous years, the suicide forest was only second in the world for highest rates of suicide, shortly behind the Golden Gate Bridge, but it has been impossible to gauge these statistics in more recent years.

This is due, in part, to the Japanese government refusing to publish any of the suicide rates of the Aokigahara Forest in recent years after the rates began climbing so high each year that the government had begun putting money and effort into stopping these occurrences. Their original idea was to prevent the publishing of the records of suicides to slowly prevent people from associating suicide with the region, in the hopes that this would prevent people from traveling to that specific region just to end their life.

This hope had proven to be a fruitless endeavor, however, as climbing rates of suicide began becoming so progressively worse that any mention of suicide or suicide statistics have become completely banned in their local media.

Interestingly enough, the Aokigahara Forest provides no extra ease in suicide. Though at the time the Golden Gate Bridge was slightly higher in its suicide rates, this was due mostly to the fact that jumping from a bridge would provide an easy and efficient way to die. The forest, however, provides no ease or efficiency and so its climbing suicide rates were originally thought to be the product of marketing and trend but after the government attempts of hiding this fact proved to be a massive failure, no theory has arisen for why it attracts so many individuals to end their life within its trees.

Number 5: Demonic Activity

Probably the most terrifying and eerie fact behind the Aokigahara Forest is its deep cultural history involving demonic presences that are referred to as Yurei by the locals. These spirits are described as dressed in pure and milky white clothing, their hair is often long, black and disheveled, their hands dangle lifelessly from the wrists of which are held outstretched with the elbows near the body, they typically lack legs or feet and are usually described as floating through the air and are frequently seen being accompanied by multiple orbs of light in eerie colors such as that of blue, green or purple.

Many people misconstrue the timing of these legends and associate these sightings as a popular lore and trend spouted due to the massive amount of suicides that occur in the forest, but this is hardly the case. Sightings of Yurei in the region go as far back as the late 17th century and predated any trends of suicide that have become popular by the mainstream media and publicized modern sightings.

These sightings have yet to cease and have shown, with the rise of suicides, to only become worse and more frequent. Many sightings today describe similar images of these Yurei and orbs of light that accompany them, including witness reports by tourists and westerners of whom are unaware of the traditional imagery of Yurei and the local folklore of such sightings. An interesting addition to this lore that concerns the appearance of Yureis and a possible explanation for their sightings is the following that is taken from a translated scripture:

"If a person dies in a sudden or violent matter such as a murder or a suicide, if the proper rites have not been performed, or if they are influenced by powerful emotions such as desire for revenge, love, jealousy, hatred or sorrow, the souls of the deceased are thought to transform into a Yurei, which can then bridge the gap back to the physical world."

Could it be possible that some form of entity is attracting people to this location to commit suicide for the sole purpose of bridging the natural world with the supernatural? Could there be some terrible entity with the goal of trying to break through and become released in our physical world? Given the sightings of such entities and the direct ties to the formation of such spirits by means of suicide, that could very well be the case.

What Happens After Death?

One of the biggest questions of life, and possibly the universe, are the questions concerning that of life after death. Though we have made many incredible and unbelievable advancements into areas that some would have believed could never be understood, we are proving to be able to go further past in technological developments than anyone could have ever hoped to have predicted.

Perhaps it is possible that one day we will be able to answer all of life's biggest questions and mysteries and these wonders of the universe will merely become nothing more than chapter 18 in a science textbook for children, but until then we are going to tackle a very daunting and possibly unexplainable question of our modern era. In this section, we will be going over 5 most likely things to happen to you after you die.

Number 1: An Afterlife

It is a common explanation for many to believe that perhaps after an individual passes away, they somehow continue to live on past their physical body and begin to experience an afterlife. There is more to this theory, however, than just the often disregarded rhetoric of age-old scriptures and religious belief.

Be it a coincidence or some form of divine intervention, nearly all religions around the world recognize an entity or variation inside the human body referred to in modern times as the soul. Judaist, Islamists, Christians, Catholics, Hindus, Buddhists and many other religions and cultures found across the globe believe the soul to be a form of pure energy that works to represent a human's consciousness and continues to live on past the annihilation of the human body. Even more interesting is this concept that highlights the belief that this soul will continue in some variation of an afterlife. A Heaven, A Hell, Uniting with a higher entity or roaming the physical universe as a spirit, the thoughts behind an afterlife can range in specific details but all hold the same core standings.

This theory of consciousness living on past the annihilation of the body has proven to be more than just a plausible theory in recent times as evidence from paranormal investigators and research scientists have been gathered. Recordings of disembodied voices, detection of electromagnetic fields with E.M.F. readers and video footage of ghostly manifestations have only helped to reinforce this theory of an afterlife.

Number 2: Reliving Your Memories

The human brain is a powerful mechanism that remains to be one of the most difficult to understand fields of study. This has led to numerous theories relative to its importance when confronting the topic of what occurs after death. Many people during a near death experience report a feeling of euphoria and of seeing their life begin to flash before their very eyes. Beautiful memories, regrets, tragedies and everything else in between begins to fill their mind as their brain begins to slowly shut down and the last of the hormones and chemicals of the brain begin to break down.

This has led to many scientific theories that hope to explain these visions of the after life and these feelings of euphoria we encounter. It has been scientifically proven that as we die, human brain activity can persist for roughly an additional seven minutes after death has been legally declared. This has led many studies to believe that, given the processing power and reports by those facing near-death experiences, the human mind can re-simulate an entire life and allow an individual to relive their life after death. Some variations of this theory can vary in their prediction of simulation and it is impossible to tell whether you are currently alive right now or reliving the memory of your life over and over again on a perpetual loop.

It is also believed that given the chemicals released during death and the euphoric feeling that can grow in an individual facing their untimely demise, that this simulation of life caused by the brain, can work to essentially slow down time to a near halt and, even though the world will continue long after you have passed away, it is plausible that you will continue to relive your life countless of times and face a temporary stasis of eternal life in the recounts of your life.

Number 3: Quantum Immortality

Advancements in quantum mechanics and within the realm of quantum physics shows that our universe may not actually be alone and that we may be one universe out of an infinite variation of parallel universes that exist. This collection of universes in quantum theory is referred to as the Multiverse and is still widely debatable to this day whether or not it truly exists. However, developments in String theory and subsequently Superstring theory believe that they have more than found proof of parallel universes existing alongside ours and that, not only do they exist, but that different variations of ourselves exist amongst them as well. This has led to the overall theory of Quantum Immortality.

Due to the fact that it might be impossible for humans to experience life after death, as death might prove to be a variation of inexistence and it is absolutely impossible for humans to experience inexistence, there is a popular belief amongst the scientific and philosophical community that you will only ever always exist in the universe where you never died.

Universes across the Multiverse do not have to follow the same rules, logics and physics of our universe, and due to this, it is mathematically plausible that out there, within the Multiverse, exists a you that will end up becoming immortal through some means or another. Let us treat this as a thought experiment. If an accident were to occur and you happened to be put in harm's way and didn't survive, if you couldn't experience life after death then your experience of that universe will cease to exist; however, in a parallel universe where you were barely out of harm's way and survived, you continued on living.

Given this possible rhetoric and thought experiment, your persistent consciousness could merely be the lucky variation of you that happened to be in the parallel universe where you lived, thus meaning that you will only ever always live in the universe where you survived and benefit from this theory of quantum immortality.

Number 4: Reincarnation

A popular belief amongst those of the Buddhist faith is the acceptance that death is merely a transformation of the body and the soul will persist in its essence and work to carry on and continue over into a new life. This act of persistence is referred to as Reincarnation by Buddhist Monks and, surprisingly enough, evidence of reincarnation exists even in the modern era.

There is none more compelling evidence than the account of Dorothy Eady. Dorothy Eady was born in London in 1904 and claims to be the living reincarnation of Om Seti, a keeper of the Abydos Temple of Seti. At birth she could fluently speak and read the Egyptian language, this was more than odd given the fact that the Egyptian language had long since been extinct and no one currently alive was aware of how it sounded.

Egyptologists would later go on to prove the legitimacy of Dorothy Eady's fluency in Egyptian, however, after Egyptologists studied native languages that arose and evolved from Egyptian in the area and found their slang and accents to directly mimic certain sounds, words and pronunciations by Dorothy Eady. This wasn't the height of her accomplishments, however, as she would later go on to help uncover many locations of Ancient Egyptian sites buried beneath sand, discover secret chambers and assist with the recovery of long forgotten and hidden Ancient Egyptian artifacts. In 1979, the New York Times wrote a piece on Dorothy Eady that regarded her as "the western world's most intriguing and convincing modern case histories of reincarnation."

Given this evidence, it is very possible that reincarnation occurs in humans and could very well be the method of continuation in life after death.

Number 5: Leaving the Simulation

Mathematicians and researchers have found that, though originally regarded as a concept that could only exist in science fiction, the odds of us all living within base reality is a billion to one. This means that mathematically speaking, it is a billion times more likely that we all currently exist in a simulation of reality rather than true reality itself. Even tech billionaire and innovator, Elon Musk, believes in this theory and has begun work in attempts at uncovering a method of leaving this supposed virtual reality.

The concept is referred to as the Simulation Hypothesis and works around the assumption that given the absolutely anomalous properties of our universe that directly mimics computational renders, we could merely be a copy of our true creators who have set us to run on a computer so that we may advance as they have and that they may understand and catalogue complex evolutionary theory.

Advancements in quantum mechanics has also proven to give this theory further legitimacy as quantum entanglement and the method of producing faster than light information theory could merely be a direct reference to render methods similarly seen in computational engines. Further concepts such as the speed of light could be merely a speed limit set on our universe to prevent crashes in the system and black holes themselves that create gravitational wells that exceed the speed of light could be these references of crashes in our simulated world.

This does not have to be a bad thing, however, as Simulation Hypothesis could very well mean that this world and this plane of existence could be nothing more than a test to prepare us for our lives outside of the simulation. It could very well mean that once our lives are finished, we may find ourselves waking up in a room someplace else with the lights coming on and our friends and family waiting for us on the other side.

Regardless of what happens after the veil of death, it is obvious that given the absolute anomalous properties of our universe and data combined that there is good reason to believe that our existence in the universe or among parallel universes will continue to persist long after out physical bodies can no longer carry us on our journeys.

Additional Information

Thank you for reading over some of my most popular articles released during my time working as a writer for one of the most popular conspiracy theory websites on the internet.

If you wish to stay up to date with information surrounding any new releases on this series or other books I have published in the past, be sure to visit www.ALSET-ORG.com to find out more. On the website you will also be able to get into contact with me via our contact page to ask any questions you have on the wide variety of topics discussed in this book or make any comments about the work overall.

Be sure to visit our page and send us an email! I always look forward to getting new letters from fans and supporters and will always try to get back to you as soon as possible! In this line of business, there's no such thing as having too many friends!